THE
FIELD OF
FIGHT

"*The Field of Fight* is a book worth reading by anyone concerned about the future security of America. It is both an engaging personal memoir by a great American soldier and military intelligence officer, General Mike Flynn, and a strategic plan by General Flynn of how to win the global war against Radical Islam and its big, power supporters. The leaders of the next American administration would benefit from reading *The Field of Fight*."

—The Hon. Joseph I. Lieberman
United States Senator, Connecticut (1989–2013)

THE
FIELD OF
FIGHT

How to Win the Global War Against
Radical Islam and Its Allies

Lt. General
Michael T. Flynn
and Michael Ledeen

St. Martin's Press ♏ New York

THE FIELD OF FIGHT. Copyright © 2016 by Michael T. Flynn and Michael Ledeen. All rights reserved. Printed in the United States of America. For information, address St. Martin's Press, 175 Fifth Avenue, New York, N.Y. 10010.

www.stmartins.com

The Library of Congress Cataloging-in-Publication Data is available upon request.

ISBN 978-1-250-10622-3 (hardcover)
ISBN 978-1-250-10623-0 (e-book)

Our books may be purchased in bulk for promotional, educational, or business use. Please contact your local bookseller or the Macmillan Corporate and Premium Sales Department at 1-800-221-7945, extension 5442, or by e-mail at MacmillanSpecialMarkets@macmillan.com.

First Edition: July 2016

10   9   8   7   6   5   4

We want to dedicate this book to all intelligence professionals who willingly sacrifice everything they have to protect and defend the United States of America.

Contents

Acknowledgments

I have so many people to thank in helping me achieve this milestone in my life. To Michael Ledeen, after our many lengthy and late night debates about the nature of the threats America faces. Michael encouraged me to put my thoughts to paper and start typing. His total commitment to this effort and dedicated support, as well as his enormously courageous and effective writing and research skills, got me through this first book, *The Field of Fight*. He helped me precisely describe my own passions, fears, and beliefs for our country and our future generations.

I also want to thank my entire family. My wife and sons, as well as their families for putting up with endless requests to read and reread, edit, and opine on critical parts of the manuscript during the rough draft period. To my other siblings, relatives, and friends for their time and contributions in helping describe and give thoughts to key aspects of my life, leading up to and over three decades of proud service in the United States military.

There are many incredibly courageous friends I also want to thank, who must go unnamed here due to their continued service to our country in the intelligence, law enforcement, and military communities. Still others who are now out of service to our country, yet served in critical assignments and places with me and believe as I do, that this country is the greatest country on the planet. But to stay strong and on top, we must remain vigilant against the relentless and steady assault on our value system as well as our way of life. A way of life I will forever be thankful for, and why I believe we must start winning again.

—Lt. Gen. Michael T. Flynn

Much of the information in this book came from those who trained, worked, and fought alongside Lt. Gen. Flynn on foreign battlefields and within the American military and defense agencies. Dozens of interviews were conducted in the second half of 2015, with the promise that interviewees' anonymity would be respected. Some of the sources were top officials, while others were junior officers, noncommissioned officers, and intelligence analysts. We thank them all for their time and their candor.

We extend particular gratitude to the late Colonel (Ret.)

Thomas O'Connell, a great American hero who suddenly and unexpectedly died while we were writing *The Field of Fight*. He will have a special place in our hearts, and in Arlington National Cemetery.

—Michael Ledeen

THE
FIELD OF
FIGHT

Introduction

In late 2005, U.S. Special Forces fighters attacked an al Qaeda safe house in central Iraq, in an operation called Objective Rivergate. We believed an important leadership meeting was taking place. It was a fierce battle, but we killed and captured most of the terrorists, and took over the house. This was the beginning of wisdom for us. The treasure trove of documents and media discovered inside a garbage bag and smelly garbage cans gave us that wisdom.

Inside the garbage containers we found extensive documentation of our enemies' knowledge and thinking. To our surprise and horror, we saw they knew a great deal about us, including the names of many local informants. They also had done a lot of planning, laying out specific objectives, the risks associated with attacking them, and the measures they should take to thwart our countermeasures.

Until Objective Rivergate, we had no idea that al Qaeda in Iraq had anything approaching that degree of sophistication. We were compelled to reevaluate our picture of the war. This was an enemy we had to take far more seriously.

Six months later we attacked another safe house, which we called Objective Larchwood. We arrived shortly after a very important meeting that had included the chief of al Qaeda in Iraq, Abu Musab al-Zarqawi. We captured a laptop computer with a video on it, showing Zarqawi himself making a Power-Point presentation to his commanders, discussing the course of the war, analyzing al Qaeda's successes and failures, ordering changes in tactics, and then leading his men in song and prayer. Zarqawi and the video were every bit as professional as anything our analysts and strategists had imagined him to be or could create.

That was ten years ago. Today Radical Islamists are fighting us on a much bigger battlefield, including our homeland (the director of the FBI has testified that he is running investigations of ISIS—the Islamic State, the successor to al Qaeda in Iraq—in every one of our fifty states). By now, we have seen numerous arrests, various attacks in our cities and against our law enforcement professionals, and young men and women being brainwashed by Radical Islamists. It is time we get serious against this vicious, barbaric enemy.

We're in a world war, but very few Americans recognize it, and fewer still have any idea how to win it.

I've been fighting for more than thirty-three years, much of the time at the top levels of U.S. military intelligence. I have some strong feelings about this war, about our "field of fight." The title comes from the ancient Greek epic poet Homer, writing in the *Iliad* about a battle involving both men and gods. Our most fanatical contemporary enemies think they are in a similar battle with us. Most of them believe their cause is blessed and supported by the Almighty. We must prove them wrong.

I wrote this book for two reasons:

1. To show you the war being waged against us. This administration has forbidden us to describe our enemies properly and clearly: they are Radical Islamists. They are not alone, and are allied with countries and groups who, though not religious fanatics, share their hatred of the West, particularly the United States and Israel. Those allies include North Korea, Russia, China, Cuba, and Venezuela.

2. To lay out a winning strategy. Any reader needs to judge the reliability of the book's author, and I'll tell you about myself so you can make an informed decision. I don't fit the stereotype most people have of a military officer, never mind a career intelligence officer. I had a successful career in the United States Army, but I'm a maverick, an atypical square peg in a round hole, as both my friends and critics will attest. My maverick direction started when I was a lot younger than I am today.

I've fought in this war on physical and bureaucratic battle-fields, from Afghanistan, Iraq, and African jungles, to the highest level of the United States' intelligence and military establishments. I know our enemies better than most "experts," and I'm plenty scared.

We could lose. In fact, right now we're losing. To make matters worse, our political leaders insist that the war is going very well, and the scores of professional analysts who know better are being censored when they report the truth to their superiors. I know this story firsthand. In 2014, I was fired as the director of the Defense Intelligence Agency after telling a congressional committee that we were not as safe as we had been a few years back.

Others who want to tell the truth about the war are fight-ing back against their censors. In the late summer of 2015, dozens of military analysts protested that their superiors at CENTCOM—the Central Command for the war in the Middle East—were blocking or altering their reports on the true course of events. That allegation was then investigated by the Penta-gon's inspector general. The story was leaked, and congressio-nal hearings were held. This book shows that the censorship isn't new; it has been going on for years, and threatens our ability to win.

I also have a lot to say about Iran, which is responsible for killing hundreds of Americans in Lebanon, East Africa, Iraq, and Afghanistan. We've known about Iran's murderous activities for many years, and you'll learn how we knew it and how the information was long suppressed by two consecutive administrations.

There's a lot of information on Iran in the files and computer discs captured at the Pakistan hideout of Osama bin Laden. Here, too, the censors have been busy. Some of it—a tiny fraction—has been declassified and released, but the bulk of it is still under official seal. Those of us who have read bin Laden's material know how important it is, and I'll tell you as much as I'm allowed.

Other information about Iran comes from the battlefield, where the Iranians have killed and maimed our troops, and continue to do so. I'll tell you how we uncovered the Iranian network in Iraq, largely by the use of spies who went back and forth between the two countries to gather the truth for us.

Then there are the terror groups, principally ISIS and al Qaeda. By now, we have seen so many horrific acts—from beheadings to crucifixions and burning captives alive—that many attentive people imagine them to be savages, barbarians. They are certainly barbaric, but they are driven by a systematic vision of how to conquer the world and impose their religious ideology on all of us. Did you know that ISIS has long worked from a detailed written timetable for global victory? It's a Radical Islamic *Mein Kampf*, and was discovered by a courageous young female American journalist in Pakistan in 2015. You'll get all the details.

We face a formidable group of terrorists and hostile countries, and we've got to be better prepared to compete or we will
need to be ready to destroy them. That requires better strategy, as well as better intelligence, to which I devoted all my
brainpower and passion for a long time. I learned how to get
accurate information, which goes hand in hand with the winning strategy, because both the information and the strategy
come from the people—the citizens of these countries—caught
up in the war itself. We must work closely with those people.
They have the crucial information, and they will determine
who wins. I changed our methods in Iraq in 2004 and in
Afghanistan starting in 2010, and they worked.

I hope to convince you that we face a potentially fatal
challenge, which we must and can overcome.

As you read these pages, remember that you don't have to
be a military officer to see the global war. A man of peace, Pope
Francis, has warned us of the gravity of our situation: "Even
today, after the second failure of another world war, perhaps
one can speak of a third war, one fought piecemeal, with
crimes, massacres, destruction," Francis said at a mass at the
Italian Military Memorial of Redipuglia. ("War Is Madness." USA-
today.com/story/news/word/2014/09/13/pope=urges-world-to-shed
-apathy-toward-new-threats/155753437).

And he knows the consequences: "War ruins everything,
even the bonds between brothers. War is irrational; its only
plan is to bring destruction: It seeks to grow by destroying."

Very few Americans—indeed very few Western leaders who, from time to time, use the word "war" and promise to "win" it—seem to recognize that a global war is being waged against us. Even the few who follow the actual combat tend to see the events separately: there's fighting in Syria, Iraq, Yemen, and the Sinai, terrorists are at work all over the place, and we try to figure out what to do in each case.

It isn't likely to work out well. Fighting well requires that you know your enemy, as the Chinese strategist Sun Tzu said. Our leaders don't want to identify our enemies. That puts us on the path to defeat.

Most Americans mistakenly believe that peace is the normal condition of mankind, while war is some weird aberration. Actually, it's the other way around. Most of human history has to do with war, and preparations for the next one. But we Americans do not prepare for the next war, are invariably surprised when it erupts, and, since we did not take prudent steps when it would have been relatively simple to prevail, usually end up fighting on our enemies' more difficult and costly terms.

So we don't know our enemy and are not prepared to fight effectively.

Fewer still have any idea how to win. I'm in a better position than most on this score. I've seen, shot, captured, interrogated, and studied our enemies.

I know them, and they scare me, a guy who doesn't scare often or easily. They scare me even though we have defeated them every time we fought seriously. We defeated al Qaeda and the Iranians in Iraq, and the Taliban and their allies in Afghanistan. Nonetheless, they kept fighting and we went away.

Let's face it: right now we're losing, and I'm talking about a very big war, not just Syria, Iraq, and Afghanistan.

We're in a world war against a messianic mass movement of evil people, most of them inspired by a totalitarian ideology: Radical Islam. But we are not permitted to speak or write those two words, which is potentially fatal to our culture. We can't beat them if we don't understand them and are afraid to define them, but our political leaders haven't permitted that. We're not allowed to use the phrase "Radical Islam" or "Islamists." That's got to change.

Once we've understood them, we've got to destroy them. Here's how:

- We have to organize all our national power, from military and economic to intelligence and tough-minded diplomacy. It's not cheap, and it's probably going to last through several generations.

- They must be denied safe havens, and countries that shelter them have to be issued a brutal choice: either eliminate the Radical Islamists or you risk direct attack yourselves. Yes, there will be some foreign countries that can't defeat their indigenous Islamists, even though they want to, and they'll need help. They shouldn't be punished twice—first by the Islamists,

then by us and our allies—and we should welcome
them to our ranks.

On the other hand, some of these countries are
considered "partners" of ours, but they aren't. We
can't afford to be gulled by foreign countries that
publicly declare their friendship, but then work in cahoots with our enemies.

- We've got to attack the Islamists everywhere and in
every way. That most certainly includes attacking
their evil doctrines and detailing their many failures.
Are we not fully entitled to tell the truth about them?
In the Cold War, we repeatedly exposed the failures of
Communism. Why shouldn't we do the same with
al Qaeda and ISIS?

As you see, I'm not a devotee of so-called political correctness. I don't believe all cultures are morally equivalent, and I
think the West, and especially America, is far more civilized,
far more ethical and moral, than the system our main enemies
want to impose on us.

This kind of war is not at all new. It created our world. I
dare say that most Americans don't realize that the religious
and political transformation of Europe that we call the Reformation entailed hundreds of years of very bloody fighting. The
religious people who settled America in the seventeenth and
eighteenth centuries were fleeing that terrible bloodshed. The

world badly needs an Islamic Reformation, and we should not be surprised if violence is involved. It's normal. The important thing is to defeat the Islamists, and we must make it clear why they have declared and waged war against us, and why we reject their doctrines.

We've got to stop kidding ourselves about the intentions of the state and nonstate supporters and enablers of violent Islamism, whether on the ground, in the mosques, or online. We speak for freedom, they denounce it and crush it. That means we are the bull's-eye at the center of their gunsights. And we've got to stop feeling the slightest bit guilty about calling them by name and identifying them as fanatical killers acting on behalf of a failed civilization.

We also have to stop kidding ourselves about our enemies' intellectual capabilities. They may be crazy, but they're not stupid. The bin Laden documents, and the ISIS timetable for victory, show they study us very carefully, and they excel at identifying our weaknesses. Once they learn how to exploit our weak points, they keep doing it. They keep staging multiple attacks against population centers, from New York City to Paris, from Mumbai to Beirut to Brussels, because it keeps working.

Finally, they are willing—sometimes eager—to die for their global mission.

So how do we prevail?

If you want to be a successful intelligence professional you have to learn how to get inside other people's minds. Mostly you're getting inside your enemies' minds, and you have to feel the same passions, beliefs, and fears that drive them. The same requirements apply to leading and following your own people, by the way. You've got to get inside the minds of both the men you lead and the ones you have to obey, whether they're military or civilians.

You've got to be able to anticipate your own men's mistakes, predict your enemies' actions, and understand what your superiors want from you. I did pretty well at the first tasks, as you can see from the results on the battlefield, and from my appointment as the highest-ranking military intelligence officer in the U.S. government. You'll have to judge for yourself how well I did in my dealings with my bosses, especially at the end of my career, when I was told my service had come to an end a year ahead of schedule.

I spent many years and a lot of effort to get inside the heads of our enemies, many of whom we killed or captured, but many of whom remain at large, hell-bent on destroying us. That's why those passions, beliefs, and fears that I found in their heads remain important today. If you understand them it's a lot easier to defeat them, which is the central mission of this generation.

We're going to have to learn to think like the evil men— women don't really count in their ranks, aside from being used to breed new killers and as suicide bombers—who have sworn homage to al Qaeda, the Islamic State, various other jihadi groups, and to the leaders of radical regimes like the one in Iran. They will continue to do terrible things, and escalate their war against us, against Muslims who reject their doctrines, against Christian "infidels," against Jews, against women, indeed against the entire Western enterprise. We have to destroy them before they fulfill their mission.

Don't think for a minute that they're not good at what they do. They have a serious ideology—replete with intense passions, beliefs, and fears—and they mean to dominate the world. They have built a fearsome movement, based on deep religious conviction. They think they're winning, and so do I.

They're good fighters. They have proven their courage and shown great skill. They learn fast, they quickly give up failing tactics, and they're skilled at the techniques of Internet operations, from hacking to propaganda. They're tough enemies, as I learned fighting them on multiple battlefields. We need to be a lot better. Today we're not nearly good enough. A big reason for that is that we don't get inside their heads. Alas, our schools, media, and social networks are doing a poor job of helping Americans understand our enemies in order to defeat them.

So is our government.

1

The Making of an Intel Officer

I was one very lucky kid. Life was rough-and-tumble for my hectic family of eleven, living and growing up in a small house in Middletown, Rhode Island. Finding a place to lay your head for a night's sleep was a never-ending revolving search to nab one of a few fold-up cots or a bunk bed that was open. And breakfast could easily turn into a negotiation or fight for the last glass of powdered milk and a piece of toast. For a time, I added to this nonstop turbulence.

Looking back, it was this turmoil and my own dangerous behavior as an adolescent that led to my ability to get inside our enemies' heads.

I was one of those nasty tough kids, hell-bent on breaking rules for the adrenaline rush and hardwired just enough to not care about the consequences. This misguided mind-set and some serious and unlawful activity by me and two of my co-hoodlum teenage friends would eventually lead to my arrest. The charges warranted a very unpleasant night in "Socko"—the state boys reformatory—and a year of supervised probation. *Saved!* I thought at the time. Stay clean for those twelve months and my record would be expunged.

As fate would have it, this arrest and my father's steel hands and mother's piercing eyes of disappointment turned my downward trajectory of crash and burn into a reservoir of opportunity for the rest of my life. From there on out, life would change. I was lucky, although it sure didn't seem that way at the time.

As the cliché goes, "it takes one to know one." Just like reformed hackers who have done tremendous work in cyber security, or the miscreants of the *Dirty Dozen* made famous in World War II for their unorthodox war-fighting ways (to say the least), I was briefly the same sort of irreverent rascal. Like many of our best intelligence professionals, life experiences, like mine, sharpen our focus into how the world looks through criminal eyes.

My father was a no-nonsense guy named Charlie. He served more than twenty years in the U.S. Army in both World War II and Korea. He retired as a sergeant first class. Like virtually all of his peers, Charlie was a tough disciplinarian and worked hard. After the Army, he went to work for a bank, starting as a teller and finishing as vice president, which tells you a lot about his talent and ambition. Common among his generation, he was a chronic smoker and like it or not, being of Irish descent, Charlie toasted life with drink in hand more than he should have done. After surviving two major heart attacks and a total of six heart bypasses, he developed serious diabetes, eventually losing both of his feet. A fighter right up to the day he died, it was a combination of smoking, drinking, heart complications, and diabetes that killed him. That day was a terrible and intense one for me. Waves of memories of my childhood rushed into my mind as I remembered the lessons I learned from my rejection of his good sergeant's counsel and near-daily physical interactions.

My mother, Helen, was an even tougher Irishman. She kept order in a one-bathroom house with nine kids who all had to be out the door at the same time. She organized the daily chaos in genealogical order, first born, first in, youngest last. It was good training for living in military barracks. In fact, growing up with enough siblings to field a baseball team was invaluable in learning how to build an effective organization of a very different kind.

Helen was valedictorian of her high school class. She was brilliant and remains the most courageous person I have ever known. Although she had received a full scholarship to Brown University's Pembroke College for women, when Charlie came back on leave from World War II and asked for her hand in marriage, she dropped out of school, married her high school sweetheart, and the kids soon started their arrivals. Later in her life, Helen went on to finish her undergraduate degree and earned her Doctor of Laws—all the time working, going to school nights and weekends while raising her Irish brood. She was not one to suffer fools gladly. And anyone foolish enough to drop by for a casual visit was immediately put to work or could find themselves in a heated political debate. She ran our house like the Army bases that were my homes for decades. Once retired from service to our country, Helen and Charlie moved into our little house on the coastline of the Atlantic Ocean in Middletown, Rhode Island, where I raised hell and drew the wrong kind of attention until these two giants in my life put a stop to it all.

One night at Socko and a year of probation were no comparison to the punishment at home. My rehabilitation was one of the fastest in adolescent history. I had it coming, and it taught me that moral rehab is possible. I behaved during my term of probation and stopped all of my criminal activity. But I would always retain my strong impulse to challenge authority and to think and act on my own whenever possible. There is room for such types in America, even in the disciplined confines of the United States Army. I'm a big believer in the value of unconventional men and women. They are the innovators and risk takers.

Apple, one of the world's most creative and successful high-tech companies, lives by the vision of transformation through exception. "Here's to the crazy ones," Apple's campaign says. "The misfits. The rebels. The troublemakers. The round pegs in the square holes. The ones who see things differently. They're not fond of rules. And they have no respect for the status quo. You can quote them, disagree with them, glorify or vilify them. About the only thing you can't do is ignore them. Because they change things. They push the human race forward. And while some may see them as the crazy ones, we see genius. Because the people who are crazy enough to think they can change the world, are the ones who do."

If you talk to my colleagues, they'll tell you that I'm cut from the same cloth.

My military biography starts badly. I was a miserable dropout in my freshman year of college (1.2 GPA), enlisted in a delayed-entry Marine Corps program, went to work as a lifeguard at a local beach, and then came the first of several miracles: an Army ROTC scholarship. Little did I know that my rebellious activities, such as skipping class and sundry other mistakes, would lead me to playing basketball (which I was very good at) with an ROTC instructor who saw something in me. Not only that, he took surprising initiative.

He came to my father's house in early August of 1978 and offered to get me a three-year scholarship if I would batten down and get better grades. And, he worked out something with the USMC to keep me from going to boot camp (to this day I don't know how he managed that one). He clearly took a risk and it clearly paid off. I wish I knew where he was today.

After completing college, I entered the Army as an intelligence officer in the field of signals intelligence and electronic warfare. Why this field and not the infantry? My professor of military science (Lieutenant Colonel O'Grady), a Special Forces officer with Vietnam experience and lots of time at a place called Fort Bragg (a place where I would spend half my career), sat me down one day and said, I know you'd do well in the combat arms, but intelligence is where you need to go. Specifically, he pointed me to this relatively new field of electronic warfare that was emerging with advanced technologies in the early 1980s. I gave it a shot on my military branch assignment requests and got in. From being a college dropout to receiving this news, I felt pretty happy that I had achieved something I would never have imagined.

My first assignment after my initial intelligence training programs—at Army bases such as Fort Huachuca, Arizona, and Fort Devens, Massachusetts, and then attending Ranger training—was the 82nd Airborne Division (America's Guard of Honor). There, I held a variety of assignments, but the most important and longest was as a platoon leader. During those formative years, I had deployments to Panama, Honduras, and other parts of Central America. In those days the United States was fighting the Sandinistas and engaging the Somozans and all manner of other insurgents in Central and South America. The Soviet Union and its allies were still our nation's main enemy and the proxy wars raged all around us.

One of those proxy wars was being played out on a tiny island called Grenada, the Isle of Spice. Although I had already done operational deployments to Panama and Honduras, along the Nicaragua border, Grenada would be my first combat deployment and combat experience. I deployed as platoon leader in support of 2nd Brigade, 82nd Airborne for operations against the Cubans who had occupied and taken over large parts of Grenada. These same forces along with the rebel militia on the island were threatening our regional neighborhood, as well as threatening a large contingent of U.S. students attending medical school on the island.

While there are differing versions of this first combat deployment, what happened was as follows:

I was 1st Platoon leader, Alpha Company, 313th Military Intelligence Battalion, 82nd Airborne Division. 1st Platoon was a Signals Intelligence Collection and Electronic Warfare Jamming platoon. For that time, it was a pretty sophisticated outfit.

The 82nd had been mobilized to go into Grenada and our intelligence battalion was part of that mobilization.

We were herding all sorts of cats during the early, very chaotic days of this operation (Operation Urgent Fury), pushing members of the battalion out through the "Green Ramp" at Pope Air Force Base in support of the division's deployment to Grenada. Once there, we had a few tasks: oust the Cubans, help the government of the now assassinated Maurice Bishop, push

Communist influence out of the Caribbean, and save the American medical students who were being held against their will.

Many of those in my Collection and Jamming platoon were exceptional Spanish-speaking electronic warfare/signals collection analysts and linguists; many were from Puerto Rico, some from Los Angeles and a couple from New York City. All were tough paratroopers who you did not want fighting against you—these young men (including myself) were well trained and always ready for a fight. That was the 82nd Airborne way and still is.

We were well prepared for any such missions, but Grenada came as a surprise, like most conflicts and wars. Although Grenada had a substantial Cuban military presence, it was better known as a vacation spot with one of the most beautiful beaches in the world—but once things started to heat up, we were besieged with calls for support. Within a few hours, members from my platoon were ordered to deploy. To be blunt, there was a lot of chaos across the division, and that certainly existed at our battalion headquarters. Our command group, under Lieutenant Colonel Tom O'Connell (universally known as "OC" and a great leader), had already deployed. He took a few men forward as a command and control element to support the division's Tactical Command Post positioned off the airfield on Grenada.

As I was being asked to deploy members of my platoon, I went to my company commander and asked for permission to deploy the remainder of my platoon, believing we could support not only current operations but any follow-on deployments that might be necessary. The reporting coming back from Grenada was a bit disjointed and the situation was confused (to be kind). And it didn't sound like things were going well.

My commander approved and at that stage I returned to the remainder of my platoon, who were all ready to go. We then arranged transportation down to Green Ramp and proceeded to get ourselves manifested on the next tranche of forces deploying into Grenada. This all happened in about a day and we finally got on an aircraft late night/early morning and arrived in Grenada at approximately first light. When we arrived, we grabbed up all of our equipment (we brought extra SIGINT and other special collection equipment) and moved to the hill overlooking the airfield where our battalion HQ was located and where I would find Lieutenant Colonel O'Connell.

He clearly wasn't aware that we would be arriving, but did immediately direct us to position our Low Level Voice Intercept (LLVI) teams on key locations around the airfield and he also directed our telecommunication intercept team to head into the city and position ourselves in the phone company, tap into the phone network, and see what we could learn. By late afternoon I, and my senior Non-Commissioned Officer in Charge (NCOIC), had moved to the phone company in downtown St. George's. We tapped into the telecommunications network on the island and started listening for Cuban communications to those trying to escape and from those on the island trying to communicate what was happening. It was a very confusing time, but looking back this was an imaginative use of paratroopers and we were able to provide some intelligence to the division and 2nd Brigade about some Cubans trying to leave the island from a coastal location. I learned later that the Navy was able to interdict a boat that was to be used to conduct the escape.

After the positioning of this element in the city, we did some rummaging around a couple of the locations that had seen fighting, and looked through some of the documents and photos that were literally strewn around the inside of these buildings and villas. We didn't find anything of real value, but it taught me how much we lost when we disregarded the kind of information that could be discovered in some of the documents, had we thought to capture them and organize them in some fashion to be of at least tactical value.

After a period of four to five days, I went back to the airfield and checked on my other Signals Intelligence Collection teams. I then positioned myself with one of my teams at the western end of the airfield—a superb location offering line of sight into the city, and along the southern and western part of the island. We could, in essence, electronically "see" and "hear" any communications.

While at this location, which was positioned along a high cliff, I was told there were men in trouble out at sea just off the coastline. I went to the cliff and saw two soldiers, who had taken a raft off the beach for a swim, but the strong currents pulled them out to sea and they were starting to panic. It was about 1700 and we had only a few hours of daylight left.

I grew up as a lifeguard and competitive swimmer from the time I could remember, and had surfed my whole life. While I always respected the ocean, I had experienced strong currents in some of the hurricanes I surfed in. Also, I had done some cliff diving as well as jumping off of a couple of pretty high bridges. One time, in my wayward days as a young radical, a Rhode Island state trooper came down to the bottom of the bridge I had just leapt from. As I swam in to shore, the trooper told me that a driver passing by said someone had just jumped off the bridge, thinking I was committing suicide. No wonder: that bridge was pretty high—probably above seventy-five feet. The trooper told me to knock it off and go home. I did, but on that day in Grenada it turned out to be a useful skill.

Meanwhile, I saw that the two soldiers were in serious trouble and one was clearly not a good swimmer, so I told my team leader to get word to the battalion that I was going to help them, and to summon additional help.

I jumped off the cliff—about a forty-foot jump into the swirling waters off the southern tip of the airfield—and swam to the two soldiers. I told them to hold on to the raft, which was deflated and no longer providing the necessary flotation to support them.

I told them I would bring each of them to the side of the cliff and place them on a ledge that we could see from the water. I decided to take one at a time and started with the weaker swimmer first. I swam each about fifty meters to the base of the cliff and, using the tide and the waves breaking up on the cliffs, pushed them to a place where they could sit and wait for more help.

There was no way that either of these guys could have made it back to shore on their own; they didn't have the swimming capability, both were very tired, and the currents were powerfully churning around the back side of the island.

I had managed to get both of them on a ledge where they were out of the water and able to get themselves composed. I stayed in the water the whole time and treaded water until more help came, while darkness was closing in.

At about sunset, a helicopter arrived to rescue the three of us. Appropriately enough, both of the soldiers were from the helicopter unit that pulled all of us out of that spot.

Since I was in the water, I was pulled up first, then the incredibly brave pararescue crewman went back down two more times to pull up the other two soldiers. This process took about thirty minutes. Once we were all on board safely, they took us over to the airfield and we then went into a medical tent and were tended to.

I had a couple of black sea urchin needles taken out of my feet, was given some vinegar to reduce the pain, bandaged them up, put my boots back on, walked over to the two soldiers I had just helped pull out of the ocean, and asked if they were okay. They both thanked me and I then headed back down to my LLVI team's position at the end of the airfield. I arrived there about 22/2300 hours; it had been a long day.

OC showed up early the next morning and asked me to walk him through what had happened (he apparently tracked it on one of the division's nets). Good to know our guys were keeping track of us!

We continued to operate for the next few days until, as quickly as the division was deployed, and in a far more orderly fashion, we flew home.

My entire time on the island lasted about a month. The operation itself was a mess, but demonstrated how badly our military needed to get better at joint operations.

I learned a lot:

- How little intelligence was paid attention to during this type of operation;
- If you're going to do this sort of operation, you either have to be overwhelming or stay home;

- Joint operations are very messy. We even had our own command and control problems within the 82nd Airborne, one of our best;
- Soldiers will rely on themselves and their leaders if they trust them. We were fortunate to have strong trust within our platoon.

I also learned to try to be patient and understanding with my colleagues. It's not so easy, but whenever I'm tempted to come down hard on someone who seems to have screwed up, I take a deep breath and think back to Lieutenant Colonel O'Connell in 1983. When I heard from OC about how my deployment was reported to him (that I had just jumped on the plane with no orders to do so), he could have relieved me on the spot. Blessedly, he looked again, and saw something he liked.

Had it not been for his patience and vision and extraordinary leadership under some difficult pressure, I'd probably be renting surfboards at Second Beach in Middletown, Rhode Island. He is where I get the quote I use routinely when I counsel young people. "A leader is responsible for helping others see something in themselves and then helping them maximize their potential." He did that in spades for me.

That said, and lest you get the impression that he's a softie, I received many a tongue-lashing from OC, and it was invariably as tough as anything I got at home. Maybe it's something about Rhode Islanders—is there an independence and toughness in the people that come from that state?

As most stories do, the Grenada story grew legs over time. Some said that I violated orders; I never did. That I jumped on an airplane to go to war; I did. That if it wasn't for the rescue of the paratroopers, I might have been court-martialed; I doubt it. . . . Believe me, an ass-chewing from O'Connell was worse than any court-martial, and he gave me many. However, our platoon performed well on Grenada. We were there for only a few weeks, and the Cubans weren't that effective at anything.

Overall, the mythology of the Flynn Deployment to Grenada would live with me for my entire career, but when I look back it was what you would expect and want of a young platoon leader. Not only were the results successful, but the experience showed me that it's vital to give your mid- and junior-level officers and Non-Commissioned Officers (NCOs) plenty of running room. They are the keys to winning modern war, as was later proven in Iraq and Afghanistan.

There's a broader point, having to do with ideologically driven regimes and movements, and it is crucial in understanding today's war. We captured a lot of documents in Grenada. They were brought back to Washington and are now in the National Archives. They tell a fascinating and important story, with great attention to little details, especially about the indoctrination of the populace and the close working relationship with Moscow (they are closely related, of course). Like the

Soviets, the Grenadian Communists were confident of their ultimate victory—the "laws of history" guaranteed it—and they wanted to be sure that their part in the story was properly told.

Today's Radical Islamists have the same conviction, and are similarly at pains to document their intentions and actions. As I told the German magazine *Der Spiegel* in late 2015, talking about the Islamic State, "They document everything. These guys are terrific about it. In their recruiting and in interviews, they ask 'What's your background? Are you good with media? With weapons?' It's this kind of well-structured capability they have that then evolves into a very, very unconventional force."

There are many similarities between these dangerous and vicious radicals and the totalitarian movements of the last century. No surprise that we are facing an alliance between Radical Islamists and regimes in Havana, Pyongyang, Moscow, and Beijing. Both believe that history, and/or Allah, blesses their efforts, and so both want to ensure that this glorious story is carefully told.

Grenada turned out to be a turning point in the Cold War because the defeat of the Communist regime there was the first time that a country had entered the Soviet Empire and was then removed from it. According to the Brezhnev Doctrine, named after the former Soviet dictator Leonid Brezhnev, once a country had embraced Communism, the laws of history dictated it could not change its political system. Grenada showed the doctrine was false.

After Grenada, I went on to serve in my first of three training assignments and my second tour at Fort Huachuca (the Army's Intelligence Center). This assignment gave me my first glimpse into future warfare. I was assigned as one of the instructors to teach intelligence in low intensity conflict and multinational operations. The time frame was in the middle of the Soviet invasion into Afghanistan and we were watching their operations like hawks—learning all we could about how the Russians were being beaten by this very difficult but what appeared to be poorly organized foe in the mujahedin, an enemy we would face almost twenty years later. I then went on to an assignment in the Pacific—the 25th Infantry Division (Tropic Lightning). This opened up my eyes to the type of enemies we saw across a wide swath of the Asia-Pacific rim. There were many, and still are. These were formative and important tactical intelligence and training and education assignments.

I was eventually promoted to major and sent back to Fort Bragg, North Carolina (where I served for over sixteen of my thirty-three-year career and at all grades, lieutenant to brigadier general). It was the summer of 1994, and things were building up again in the Caribbean on another island, this time Haiti, which we would address under Operation Uphold Democracy.

I was the chief of war plans working for the G3, Director of Operations, of the 18th Airborne Corps, eventually working for an officer by the name of Colonel Dan K. McNeill, who went on to be a four-star general. I was lucky enough to work for him three more times in very critical and impactful assignments later in my career. If there was one officer who had the *most* impact on my success in the Army, it was General McNeill—bar none. He still stands as one of our most combat-capable senior leaders and one who was respected across the entire joint force—achieving four stars having never served in the Pentagon—an amazing example of leadership and high moral character.

The commanding general of the corps at the time was Lieutenant General Hugh Shelton, who would go on to become chairman of the Joint Chiefs of Staff. He was a superb commander.

We planned the final parts of the operation to seize Haiti's airfield and subsequently fight the Haitian military (a third-rate group of thugs), as well as some Cubans who were also on the island. It was a real mess, but this was my first taste of Joint and Multinational and Unconventional Operations at the joint task force level.

Haiti is a miserable place in many ways, but I had a great experience. I learned an enormous amount about how to view intelligence while deployed in combat, far more than I saw as a platoon leader in Grenada. I learned about integrating intelligence with operations, I learned about how a small insurgent force could hold off a much larger and more organized military simply due to knowing the indigenous and physical terrain, and I learned just how poorly the U.S. intelligence community was set up to support war fighting. We got very little from "national intelligence," something that I would see years later in a place called Iraq.

After returning from this Haiti deployment, I was called in for what I expected would be a routine meeting with Colonel McNeill. Surprise! He told me I was going to be assigned to Fort Polk down in Louisiana, a place known locally as "Snake Central," because of the abundance of wildlife. At the time, this was very unusual. I hadn't been back in Bragg more than six months and here I was being told I'm going to move. He told me to go see the G1 (head of personnel), who would explain everything. I thought I was being exiled.

There had been an unexpected shake-up at Fort Polk. The senior intelligence trainer was being relieved of duty and I was going to replace him. Looking back, there were two unusual things about this: one, the position normally went to a lieutenant colonel and former battalion commander, someone with much more experience than I had (I was still a young major), and two, I was being reassigned with less than a year on station from one base inside the United States to another. Normally assignments of a year or less would be to places like Korea . . . but unusual things happen, so I went home to inform my wife we were being assigned to Fort Polk (she almost killed me).

Again, one learns different things throughout one's career.

For me, this experience taught me about myself, my family, my abilities, and gave me a renewed sense of confidence in our Army and our institution. This is all hindsight; at the time, I thought my career was ending and we would live out our days at Snake Central.

However, the assignment to Polk turned out to be game changing for me. I had the honor and privilege to observe, and work alongside, some of our very best military leaders (and, alas, some of our very worst). Among the best were men like then Colonels Stan McChrystal, Dave Petraeus, and J. R. Vines (retired three-star and commander of the International Security Assistance Force, ISAF, in Afghanistan). You couldn't work alongside such giants without developing a passionate commitment to do everything possible to give them everything they needed to win, and from my standpoint it was evident that on-the-ground intelligence and our overall intelligence system just weren't giving them what they needed.

We were overwhelmingly focused on big tank battles and still trying to get past the Soviet Union, seeking an enemy that would fight us on the plains of somewhere. Our Army found it hard to change and the intelligence system was no different. We were planning and training for big land battles as in World War II, even though we'd been badly beaten up in Vietnam by a well-organized network. There were many late-night discussions at Polk about how to fight against guerrilla forces, breaking the connectors that made them an effective network, and then destroying them piece by piece. This was the beginning of the development of a truly effective system to win such wars. It required much better technology, a greatly increased tempo of activity by our forces, more skilled and operationally savvy intelligence officers, interrogators, and fighters, and a new approach to battle: decentralizing decision making in order to put the talents of American soldiers to their maximum effectiveness.

The bottom line was that intelligence would be vastly more important. And there I was!

This new approach took formal shape under Stan McChrystal in Iraq over a decade later. It's what enabled his Task Force 714 to do so well. But it didn't happen quickly, and it really didn't get going until we realized we were losing in Iraq. The pieces were plugged in one at a time. Among the things I brought to the intelligence system for the joint force, and to those commanders rotating through Fort Polk's elite training center, was a rarely used approach that turned out to be crucial for the next two decades of war fighting. It was simply called "Pattern Analysis."

Pattern Analysis is a very detailed form of intelligence work that requires the complete breakdown of an enemy's cell structure, much like a doctor would break down a disease to find a cure. As I look back on my two years of training twenty combat brigades at Fort Polk, this type of work would eventually pay off when we started fighting al Qaeda and its ilk.

One thing more on this assignment to the Joint Readiness Training Center at Fort Polk: I learned how ineffective our human intelligence and interrogation operations were. They were essentially nonexistent, poorly executed (if at all), and had to be scripted into the live training that we did. I resolved to fix it, but such intelligence wasn't taken seriously until we got to Iraq—and made serious errors in judgment at a place called Abu Ghraib that still impact us today—and started losing.

We had a long way to go, but no matter how brilliantly we organized ourselves, no matter how accurate our focus might be, the fundamental requirement for good intelligence was and is total commitment to the truth. I know this seems obvious; any sensible American realizes that bad information will automatically lead to bad decisions, bad strategy, and likely defeat. Yet some of our most famous intelligence officers, military or civilian alike, have found ways to rationalize the production of seriously misleading information for our policymakers. If you want to see how it works, maybe in greater detail than you have time for, have a look at that small masterpiece about intelligence during the Vietnam War, *War of Numbers*, written by a CIA analyst suitably named Sam Adams.

Adams carefully studied our intelligence on the Vietcong, and found that if the numbers were correct, there were very few of them left, since the number of deaths and desertions greatly exceeded the level of recruitment. This was palpably false, and Adams relentlessly exposed the nonsense for the better part of ten years, all to no avail. CIA and the military had their numbers—numbers that showed we were winning the war—and would not change them.

Adams was right, but the official numbers were endorsed over and over. How could this be?

Part of the answer is that the intelligence community was not being honest about the gains that President Lyndon Johnson and the commanding generals (William Westmoreland was the most famous) were claiming to the public: Vietcong shrinking, America winning. So even when Adams and others presented more accurate data—showing the enemy was much stronger than we admitted—it was dismissed.

Nowadays we call this "politicization of intelligence," but its older name is "don't deliver bad news to your leaders." You don't want to be that messenger. And so you just keep quiet. This is what appears to be going in our intelligence system today regarding our fight against Radical Islamists—and it all starts at the very top of our government. The president sets the tone and the priorities. This doesn't surprise me. The policy-makers in the administrations of both George W. Bush and Barack Obama did not want bad news either. This was partic-ularly evident concerning Iran's role in the war.

As I look back, at least President Bush finally realized that we were losing the war against al Qaeda in Iraq (AQI) and he decided to change our strategy. Despite other strategic errors in judgment by his administration, this shift in strategy and significant changes of leaders allowed us to win in Iraq. But to no avail, because winning is only temporary if you don't sustain your success. Everyone that has paid attention to the unraveling of the situation in the Middle East realizes today the tragic error in judgment when President Obama made the fateful decision to pull out our forces in Iraq in 2011. This decision led to the rise of the Islamic State and the significant and dangerous increase in Iran's proxy war involvement across the region and its near-takeover of Iraq as a surrogate.

Intelligence is a tough business. Most information I gave to my commanders over my many years as an intelligence officer was bad news. You develop a resiliency, and you also develop a knack for taking one for the team—but thankfully, I worked for superb leaders during most of my career, who respected my judgment and my advice.

That said, I detest those who distort the truth in order to make their superiors happy. Neither I, nor my colleagues, played that game. In the end, we were able to devise a winning strategy against AQI because we were willing to face the truth even when it was unpleasant. As I said early on, I was always comfortable being a square peg that could not fit comfortably in its assigned round hole. I remained a maverick to the very end.

2
War Fighting

The Iraq War was the template for what followed in Afghanistan and Syria. Although we were in Afghanistan first and initially "won," Iraq became the main effort—the priority. Once that happened, we lost sight of what we needed to do in Afghanistan. Despite the great commanders and soldiers we were sending into that theater, Iraq quickly came to consume everything. Practically all resources (at least the good stuff) were diverted to fight an enemy that had nothing to do with the attacks on 9/11. And our enemy was not a foreign army in the conventional sense of war fighting. This was a guerrilla war. The enemy was an extensive network of combatants out to kill us. We were up against a checkerboard of Iraqis, foreign fighters primarily from Arab countries enlisting local tribes, and Iranian killers and intelligence operatives providing the training, funding, and weapons to their friends in Iraq.

We were unprepared for this revolutionary battle.

Our commanders and soldiers needed to know, in granular detail, who we were up against. They needed a clear understanding of the mash-up enemies' interaction. Were we fighting the remnants of Saddam Hussein's Baathist state? Was this a national uprising against us, or an alien occupying force? Were there national leaders, or were there so many tribal, ethnic, religious, and regional divisions within the country that we needed very different tactics to establish order?

In traditional warfare, armies determine the winner and loser of battlefield conflict. One side wins and the other side surrenders. There is a victor and a vanquished. Not so in a guerrilla war where, counterintuitively, the better you do—the more enemies you kill and capture—the worse things can get. Just look at the Soviets in Afghanistan. They killed countless Afghan and foreign jihadis. When it was over, there were more enemy fighters than before. Why? The jihadis say that if we kill one of them, ten new fighters rush to fill the void.

As unconventional as the Iraq War was, we mastered it. Afghanistan was a different story. We knew that the Soviets had killed a lot of Afghans, but by the time of their retreat they had created a larger insurgency. It obviously wouldn't do to simply kill our enemies, even their top leaders. The French had learned this in Algeria and we had some prior experience that confirmed the lesson in the Philippines and Vietnam.

The basic principle of guerrilla warfare is that the people

on the ground determine the outcome of the conflict. And when I say "the people on the ground," I'm not talking about the terrorists. I'm talking about the resident population. These are the people who will eventually choose the winner and the loser. Their decision is dependent on us getting the information we need from them for our war fighters to use, and gaining their support. And their choice depends on several other factors that determine which way they go.

First and foremost, the population does not want to get dragged into the fighting at all. They will stay out as long as they can, until *they decide* which side is destined to win. Only then are their battle lines drawn.

Notice two things: their decision is not primarily a political, let alone a moral, preference; and the decision is a self-fulfilling prophecy. That's because they choose their side once they decide who the winners-to-be are. Once they throw their support in that direction, that side gains an unbeatable advantage because "support" means the winners-to-be have the critical intelligence and the indispensable manpower they need to win.

Not that there is no political element involved in this crucial decision; it's there, but the brutal realities of the war overwhelm their political preferences. Many Iraqis, especially the Sunni tribal leaders in Anbar Province, joined us because they were disgusted by the savagery of al Qaeda. Ironically, they may not have preferred, or even liked, the side they supported. But once convinced it's the winning side, information flows and support follows. Machiavelli was right when he analyzed this type of strange environment: "It is better to be feared than loved, if you cannot be both."

Furthermore, the context for picking sides is local, not national or even chosen by regional governments. The decision is made by tribes, clans, and networks. Indeed, the people in one location often made decisions directly contrary to their nearby neighbors just down the road. In practice, it could mean supporting Sunnis in one place and Shi'ites in another.

We weren't accustomed to thinking in such a way or acting accordingly. We had to change our strategic war-fighting approach. Above all, we had to mesh with the locals. In practice, this meant that the primary focus of the war had to fundamentally shift from ground fighting to intelligence operations. This doesn't mean killing ended, it simply required a completely different and far more precise attitude to warfare.

The Cold War was a bad model for winning the war in the Middle East. In the Cold War, the Soviet Union was tough to penetrate, and recruiting good informers was difficult and dangerous. But in Iraq and to a lesser degree Afghanistan, we were deployed all over the place, and could talk to most anyone. Eventually, we infiltrated the enemy's networks. Sometimes this turned out to be extraordinary intelligence—bulletproof intelligence, in fact. We ran informants, we ran deception operations, we ran counter-information operations, and we also ran extremely effective interrogation operations. All of these operations required very simple but very smart technology. However, and more important, they required physical and intellectual courage, superb intelligence analysis, and some really savvy, cunning special operators who understood the enemy and the human geography we were facing at that time.

The breakthrough came in Anbar Province in Iraq, which provided the model for the Surge of U.S. forces, and later shaped our strategy in Afghanistan. In war, things change all the time, and dramatic changes are often overlooked. This is what happened in Iraq in 2006. In the summer of 2006, the Marines prepared a report on the situation in Anbar, which borders on Syria, from which large numbers of foreign terrorists entered Iraq. The Marines' report was written at a time when Anbar was the bloodiest province in the country and Ramadi was the most violent city. In one report I will never forget, there were over 1,500 AQI terrorist-related murders in the month of July alone.

Looking back, in late spring of 2006, it was hard to see how this situation could be reversed, especially since requests for additional Marines were denied by the Department of Defense. According to a detailed "lessons learned" analysis by the Marine Corps, top American leaders, including CENTCOM commander General John Abizaid and Multi-National Force-Iraq (MNFI) commander General George Casey, had come to believe that the presence of American armed forces was the cause of the uprising. Believing this, the generals ordered the troops to lay off the cities and hunker down in their forward operating bases in preparation to moving out. Generals Abizaid and Casey had essentially thrown their arms up in the air, and the intelligence report on Anbar reflected their position. When selected parts of the report were leaked to *The Washington Post*, the generals described the province as "lost."

The reality was that despite having the most sophisticated military machine in the history of warfare, we were losing the war in the summer of 2006. We knew it—but some simply could not admit it. The senior leadership began to sense it and I could feel it during many of the briefings I attended, including a major gathering in late summer of 2006 at MNFI HQ. There were so many necessary decisions made that late summer and early fall to change the course of the war that history has already documented and don't need to be recounted here. But to me, the most important decision came from the White House under President Bush. He realized the war was going badly, that we were losing, and our entire strategy needed to change. The mere fact that he recognized this and proceeded to make the difficult decisions he eventually made is a leadership characteristic our current president lacks.

President Bush not only changed the strategy, but he changed the commander in Iraq, brought in General David Petraeus and, even more important, he brought in Dr. Robert Gates to be the secretary of defense. These two men changed the direction of the war and the situation was reversed within the next two years.

Some in the media marveled at this amazing turnabout. Associated Press reporter Michael Fumento wrote:

> How can it be that last year AQI fled the province and now we've handed military control of pacified al Anbar to Iraqi forces, in what the AP properly described as "a stunning reversal of fortune"? Further, how could this have occurred just two years after the Marines, who were in charge of Anbar military operations, admitted in a classified report that "there is almost nothing the U.S. military can do to improve the political and social situation" and we were "no longer able to defeat a bloody insurgency" or "counter al Qaeda's rising popularity." (http://fumento.com/military/anbar.html)

It certainly looks like an intelligence failure. Here is how the Marines saw it in retrospect from an account by Major Alfred R. Connable.

> By the middle of '06, Ramadi essentially looked like Stalingrad. We were dropping shells in the middle of the city. . . . It was a disaster at that point. I argue that mid-2006, the population had recovered from the blow of the destruction of the first Awakening, and they had reached the culminating point with al-Qaeda. They had reached the point with al-Qaeda where

they had had enough. So now you had, at a very broad level, the people—not everybody, but the people, a majority of the people in Anbar—were ready for a change. A lot of them were ready to come in our direction, and you saw a change in rhetoric, and I got this because I was reading all the traffic every day and engaging with people. Guys that in 2004 were saying, "Get out, get out of the cities. We'll take control of everything," were saying, "You need to secure the cities for us, and then leave." You saw pockets of resistance against al-Qaeda. (www.marines.mil/Portals/59/Publications/Al-Anbar%20 Awakening%20Vol%20I_American%20Perspectives%20%20 PCN%2010600001100_1.pdf, p 133ff)

Fair enough, but if "a majority of the people in Anbar were ready for a change," we should have seen it, and acted accordingly. Instead, we produced an evaluation of the situation in Anbar that was misleading.

Some people will tell you that the Marines' information was out of date. That if they had written the report a few months later, it would have been closer to the reality on the ground. I don't believe that. They did intelligence correctly. U.S. intel officers and our operators were out in the field, talking to people, getting a sense of what was going on. The failure was political. We had plenty of information, but we didn't get the picture totally right. It wasn't an analytic failure; in my opinion, it was driven—as so many intelligence failures are—by a policy failure from the top ranks. Our senior officers had wrongly concluded that we were the cause of the uprising in Iraq. Therefore, when the Marines asked for more troops, our senior leaders—notably General Casey, the CENTCOM brass, the Joint Staff, and many of Defense Secretary Donald Rumsfeld's advisors—weren't inclined to approve the request. The only people who insisted that additional Marines could make a big difference were the Marines themselves. They knew.

A similar failure is happening today with ISIS and al Qaeda. There's plenty of information, but it conflicts with the "narrative" of our policymakers. When politicians are wedded to an unreal story line for their own convenience and purpose, the intelligence gets suppressed or bottled up. One disastrous outcome of this willful decision making is the 2015 intel scandal at the United States Central Command in Tampa. This scandal, in which senior military and political officials were accused of ignoring, suppressing, or rewriting intelligence analyses about Afghanistan, is an alarming indicator of policy overreach into a system that must provide truth to power. There can be no winks, no nods, there must be brutal truth telling. Those intelligence personnel who give in to their own personal weaknesses and who are overly cautious because they fear an ass-chewing or worse, are being beyond irresponsible. In combat, their weakness results in loss of life and national defeat.

Once these changes in Iraq occurred, we did better in

Anbar and then throughout Iraq. We had a base at al-Qaim on the Syrian border, where the Marine Corps was trying to block the movement of foreign fighters into Iraq—who were there to kill us—and the flow of Iraqi oil into Syria that was enriching the tyrannical regime of Bashar al-Assad. We were not permitted to cross the border into Syria, even in "hot pursuit" of terrorists, and we eventually figured out that it was necessary to work with local tribes. The tribesmen did not have the same restrictions we did. They lived and operated on both sides of the border. In time, the locals learned that it was better to work with U.S. Marines than with Syrian intelligence. We paid more than the Syrians, so business was a lot better with us. We were not Islamists and therefore did not impose a rigid political or ideological doctrine on tribal areas. In addition, the Marines were vastly better fighters, and it soon became apparent to the locals that we were not going to be defeated.

One early indicator that we could turn this situation around came on the night of November 2, 2006. Our task force conducted a raid to capture a senior al Qaeda leader in Iraq. He was known to us as the Commander of the North. This meant he was in charge of Iraq's northern sector, including large parts of the Anbar region, everything north of Baghdad, all the way up to the major city of Mosul. He was a big ticket. Due to some exceptional human intelligence and exquisite interrogation work on the part of our interrogators and intelligence analysts, our operators captured him in his home. Like many

AQI leaders we captured, he started to talk almost immediately. By this time, our interrogators had become exceptional and could move information so fast between our intelligence system and our operators that it was a dazzling thing to behold. The Commander was shocked that we seemingly knew more about his own life and activities than he knew about himself. In a matter of a few nights, we pulled out of him the locations of eighteen other AQI leaders that were subordinate to him.

After only a few nights of interrogations, and with a superb lay down of intelligence and human-targeting information, a decision was made to execute a large-scale operation to capture or kill all of the subordinate leaders. Late November (approximately Thanksgiving), in one period of darkness, our task force operators conducted a series of raids. These raids resulted in all eighteen commanders being captured. Our special operators are amazing and brave warriors—the best of the best. The level of precision they applied, the fact that there were practically no firefights against the capture of any of these AQI commanders, and the intelligence gained from this operation gave us an overwhelming sense that, if we were able to sustain pressure against their networks, we could beat these guys, hands down!

As our cooperation with local tribes increased, they learned that they had been lied to about our intentions in their country. They had been told that we were imperialists, and that we had come to colonize Iraq. As we worked together, they saw that we had no desire to live in that godforsaken place, and would go back home once we had fulfilled our mission. On the other hand, we were resolved to win, and were not about to suddenly turn tail and leave them to their own destiny. Both convictions were necessary for effective collaboration: we had to be seen as temporary occupiers, not colonialists, and they had to be convinced that we would fight alongside them until we had won—together.

We established close working relations with the Sunnis in Anbar. Not only the sheikhs who led the tribes, but their people began to believe that we were there to help and their interests and beliefs became our interests and beliefs. Never mind sending our guys to their relatively secure forward operating bases, as our top brass desired; we had to do the opposite. Indeed, we had to flip the way we waged war. We had to invert the relative weight of military operations and intelligence; that is, by treating Iraq (and later Afghanistan) as an intelligence war.

Before my eventual assignment to work for General McChrystal, I visited Iraq and Afghanistan in early 2004 to get acquainted with his command (Task Force 714), his team, and their current operating style. It was efficient but not effective, and General McChrystal knew it. After a couple of weeks, I came to recognize that this organization had a formidable capability, but they didn't have the intelligence that they needed. They weren't even considering it to the degree that they should have. They were focused on traditional targeting, above all, the top level of the terrorist groups (the so-called high-value targets). Capturing and killing top-tier terrorist leaders made us feel good, but it was a failed strategy.

We had an intense one-on-one discussion one night in Bagram, Afghanistan. Stan was deciding to transfer his HQ team and the task force's main effort from Afghanistan to Iraq, which was not a small decision—it was April of 2004 and the First Battle of Fallujah was raging and we were losing. Osama bin Laden was still on the run somewhere in Pakistan, the situation in Afghanistan was relatively stable, but underneath this deceptively calm river of Afghanistan was a raging insurgency getting ready to reemerge. A decision had to be made and Stan's instincts, as usual, were correct. That evening, I said to him, "Your intelligence operations are a small part of your organization and they need to be 80 percent of what you do as an organization. It needs to be the majority of what the task force does because, frankly, what we are facing we don't know squat about."

We had to put together a million-piece puzzle and had no box top to look at to help us. The puzzle was massive and it was in a region of the world and against an ideology that we did not properly understand. The more we tried to place the enemy in a typical conventional box, the more they changed. The more we tried to apply old, twentieth-century tactics, techniques, and procedures to this enemy, the more they adapted to them. We needed to act faster than they could and the only way to do that was to get inside their heads. And an intelligence officer who says he's inside the head of the enemy is lying if he isn't either dealing with a former enemy who's come over to our side, or he's talking directly to them and discovering what makes them tick.

This was so important that I couldn't just delegate the task. I personally got involved in many interrogations and debriefings, especially early on. I wanted to know if the evil I could imagine was sufficient for full understanding, or if I was underestimating this enemy. For many years as an intelligence officer, I always believed that if I could think it, the enemy could think it. And I came to think about some pretty evil things—maybe it was the way I grew up or maybe it came from watching movies or maybe it was just instinctual on my part. But we were facing a despicable foe, one who would rape and pillage women and children, boys and girls, behead for fun, all while watching pornography on their laptops. In fact, at one point, we determined that 80 percent of the material on the laptops we were capturing was pornography. These sick, psychopathic foes were unbelievably vile, but they were also guileful and cunning. If we were to beat them, we needed to outwork and outwit them.

How did we do it?

Let's say we captured somebody who knew something

important. That information went at once to everyone in the task force: analysts, interrogators, SIGINT personnel, and the guys in the field. Everyone could then pursue new linkages in the terror network, leading to new captures, new discoveries of documents, computers, and the like. Faster and faster, those discoveries went back into our decision loop. Once we figured out how to do it, interrogators could receive real-time information about which they could query their captives, and if the answers pointed to new action, that would be relayed back to the tacticians and fighters.

It couldn't have been done without improved communications technology. Paradoxically, al Qaeda and other terrorist groups understood this very well, and developed new skills using Internet sites to communicate with one another. We had to play catch-up. We're a lot better today than we were then, thanks in no small measure to the work we did in Iraq first, and then in Afghanistan, but these skills are perishable if not routinely used.

That said, this was collaborative, transparent intelligence sharing in a more rapid fashion than warfare had ever seen. General Stan McChrystal was the principal driver of this revolutionary intelligence system, and thus turned Task Force 714 into an unprecedented instrument of modern intelligence warfare. He allowed me and my intelligence team complete autonomy when it came to crafting innovative techniques and procedures to rapidly transfer knowledge on one of the most complex and dangerous battlefields we had experienced in decades.

Our objective was to ensure that when one of our special operations teams captured someone, they received immediate feedback. When I arrived, guys we captured were just being dropped off, large bags of captured "stuff" were being thrown into a closet, never to be exploited for intelligence, and we were simply too slow. That was it! This would never allow us to understand all the dimensions of this field of fight we were on.

I wanted to amass information against the enemy we were capturing on the battlefield. The only way to defeat them was to get to know them better than they knew themselves, and we did. As we spoke to multiple detainees (many senior members of AQI and even those al Qaeda captured in Afghanistan or in friendly Arab countries like Jordan), we began to clarify the one-million-piece puzzle of this very effective enemy we were facing.

In Iraq, we got them to talk about each other. We would then go back and verify things on the battlefield. We would use unmanned surveillance to check on things we were learning in the interrogation booth, and we would direct human sources to go check out what we learned from these guys.

All of that led us to get smarter and then move faster than they could cope with. This was fusion of intelligence in the interrogation process with advanced communications technology and effective operations on the battlefield. In the end, we operationalized intelligence to increase knowledge for our tactical to strategic decision makers. This type of intelligence warfare was and remains a critical component of how to destroy Radical Islamism today and those enemies we will face in the future.

As you can see, interrogations were enormously important, and as the new system evolved, we increased the number and quality of our interrogators. All our hard work led to a new kind of intelligence system that constantly meshed with our actions. Intelligence had to drive operations, if possible within a single day, because the terrorists were very fast. For us to dominate the battlefield, our fighting teams must have the most significant and up-to-date intelligence so they can pinpoint their next logical attack. For that to happen, we couldn't do intelligence the old way; there simply wasn't time for the information to move through the various bureaucratic levels, nor could our fighters wait for guidance. We had to do something quite different: the intelligence people had to be linked together with our operators, and they had to get the results of their fighting almost immediately.

There was still more to do. We needed to get rid of the bureaucratic bottlenecks, within our task force and more broadly within the various military services, and perhaps most difficult, between the three-letter intelligence agencies that were working, analyzing, and fighting, but doing so in their own stovepiped systems: National Security Agency (NSA),

Central Intelligence Agency (CIA), Defense Intelligence Agency (DIA), and so forth. This meant undoing the traditional chain of command, because our men in the field had to be able to act on the intelligence they were getting. The terrorists were fast, and we had to be faster.

Two examples bring this need for speed to light. The first is the use of a national jewel called the National Media Exploitation Center (NMEC) located in Washington, D.C. This organization was doing some amazing work. They were taking captured material and turning it around to us as fast as they could (in days and weeks at that time—and this was fast—but it had to be faster). Between myself, and then-director of NMEC Roy Apselof, we figured out a way to build an "electronic bridge" directly between NMEC in Washington and our task force HQ in Balad, Iraq. Once we got this "bridge" in place, we exponentially sped up our exploitation process and turned information around, now in minutes and hours instead of days and weeks. This adaptation broke through so many layers of bureaucracy, was done without orders and long bureaucratic processes or permission, and helped us accomplish our mission. It was accomplished only through personal relationships; sadly, the entire war had to be fought like this. Left to its own traditional devices, the bureaucracy, at all levels and, maddeningly, at every opportunity, would crush adaptation and ingenuity.

The second example was more tactical but just as effective.

In the early days during interrogations we would bring paper maps into the interrogation booth. The maps would be used with the detainees to get them to point out locations of certain places we were interested in finding out about. One day, we were sitting around talking about the use of Google Maps by some of our operators and tactical units because the larger imagery system wasn't working fast enough to respond to our requirements. Google Maps was a relatively new technology and a software that was available on the open market. One of our great interrogators asked, "Why can't we use this technology during interrogations?" Instead of asking why, we turned the question into "Why not?" So we did. And at first, we did Google 101: we literally taught detainees how to use a mouse with a laptop. Then we went Hollywood and put up large, flat-panel screens in the interrogation booths. Overnight, we got exponentially more fidelity of the locations we were interested in and much more accuracy for our targeting. Better still, the detainees actually liked using it. It seemed fun to them, it reinforced their fears and suspicions that the Americans knew everything and could see everything, and it made the interrogations faster. The resulting information could be electronically tracked from the interrogation booth, right out to the analytic floor, and in a digital flash right down to the operators on the battlefield.

It was an amazing application of technology, and shows you that real innovation can be conjured up by smart, highly motivated American soldiers on a battlefield. We were trying to save our operators' lives, destroy our enemies, and win the damn war. To do this, our network had to be faster, more agile, and more relentless than the enemy network we were facing. We were, and that is why we eventually won.

In sum, Task Force 714 was drastically transformed. To be an effective action arm, the operational units had to be coordinated with a robust intelligence capability comprising several of the three-letter agencies of the intelligence community. Actionable intelligence had to lead the way in the fight against AQI—that was then and remains the case now.

Interestingly, pushing our decision making down into the midlevel officer and NCO ranks mirrored our overall strategy of moving out of our secure bases and immersing ourselves in the society. While we never stopped our hunt for the terrorists' top leaders—Zarqawi headed the Most Wanted List until we finally killed him—we worked harder and harder to dismantle the terror network. This meant that our midlevel leaders tracked down their action officers at the core of the AQI network. Once we learned how to do it, it was really no contest. Good as the terrorists were, our guys were better trained, better equipped, and were part of a better, faster, and more devastating network.

Sometimes we got super-lucky and captured men who came over to our side. Or pretended to. I generally preferred to capture the terrorists in Iraq and Afghanistan, hoping to recruit some of them to our side. My youthful sortie into violent misbehavior had taught me that some criminals can be brought over from the dark side, but many of the terrorists that we did capture wouldn't convert. Members of the Islamic State, the bad guys in the Taliban, and al Qaeda in Iraq, the vicious killers who reported to Abu Musab al-Zarqawi, often proved unreformable. To make our task even more difficult, lots of them were gifted fakers, and jumped back and forth from our side to the terrorists. They fooled a lot of us, me included.

There are many examples of terrorists who pretended to cooperate, while they were actually betraying us. One, we'll call George, due to Department of Defense censorship, was one of the earliest examples. He was in Zarqawi's inner circle and in early fall 2004 we discovered he was one of the runners for AQI. This meant he had direct access to Zarqawi and his henchmen, all of whom were prime targets for us. If we could grab him, and convince him to work with us, the payoff might be enormous. So we mounted a major operation to accomplish this, and after several failures we captured him one night in a bar.

By that time, our interrogators had gotten much better, and I had developed considerable confidence in their findings and recommendations. I was delighted to hear from them, and after a few interrogations I was informed that George was coming around. I was asked by our HUMINT team (human spies, as opposed to SIGINT, or intercepted communications), for permission to put him back out on the battlefield as an intelligence source. The team felt strongly that he would work for us.

We took the risk. Later on, we would have gone much slower, but at that point we had very little good HUMINT targeting Zarqawi's inner circle and practically no overhead ISR (Intelligence, Surveillance, and Reconnaissance) or even good SIGINT.

It started well. George provided us with some good intel for a few weeks, stretching into approximately three months. It was basic information, precisely what we needed to target the al Qaeda network: safe houses, IED locations, names and identities of other AQI operatives. Then suddenly we received word from another detainee that George had been involved in a meeting with Zarqawi himself and he had not reported this to us. Nothing more devastating could be imagined, and it checked out. Worse yet, he somehow realized that we were on to him, because when we reached back out, he did not show up. We did that multiple times over about a week. He'd fooled us.

Once we established he was back on the side of Zarqawi, we knew we had to hunt him down to either capture or kill him. He was inside our detention system, so he knew how we were working to turn detainees and we could not afford to have him out there talking too much. If the terrorists knew our methods, they could outwit us just as George had.

We made it a priority to find him, partly to try to convince him to come back—an unlikely long shot to be sure—but mostly because it was terribly dangerous to have such a man on the loose. He knew too many things about our methods, after all, and we didn't want him educating Zarqawi's men. They were tough enough without giving them an additional helping hand.

We found him one night in Fallujah in early winter 2005. He and a couple of others were hiding in a house in the city. It was too dangerous for our operators to go in after them. The intelligence was excellent that evening. We were certain he was in the house, and we decided to destroy the building and kill all inside. We did.

We had no regrets about killing George and his cronies. Having him off the street was a good thing and it sent a message to our enemies that we would hunt down anyone that turned his back on us.

Our whole team had every reason to be proud of our accomplishments in Iraq, but some credit has to be given to the terrorists. They had the upper hand on several occasions and in several different areas, which according to the rules of guerrilla war should have produced victory. It didn't, for several good reasons:

- They unleashed unprecedented violence on the local populations (keep in mind that Saddam was plenty violent but the terrorists were even more so);

- They proved unable to cope with our strategy, and starting in places like Anbar Province in Iraq in 2007 and Helmand Province, Afghanistan, in 2010, the local tribal leaders and their people could clearly see that;

- They were exposed as liars regarding us. When we invaded Iraq in 2003, al Qaeda and their supporters told the Iraqi people that we had come as the latest wave of foreign imperialists, and that we intended to add them to the masses of people around the world subject to the American imperium. We weren't doing so, of course, we just wanted to win and go home. As they got to know us better, the Iraqis recognized they had been deceived.

General McChrystal tells an important story in his memoir. It's about a conversation between one of the very finest British special operators, Lieutenant General Sir Graeme Lamb, and his favorite detainee, Abu Wail, the religious emir of Ansar al-Sunnah (aligned with AQI, mostly made up of Iraqis too), which was a significant element in the uprising against us. There were very bad vibes between the two; as McChrystal says, "given half a chance, the emir would saw Graeme's Scottish head off." But they talked every couple of weeks, and Wail was treated with respect: he was taken out of his orange prisoner garb, dressed in traditional clothes, his handcuffs and chains were removed, and there was a full teapot. The epiphany came very quietly:

> *"You know," he said matter-of-factly, "you're a force of occupation, and don't try to tell me differently. That's how we see it—and you are not welcome." He explained to Graeme . . . that guidance from the Koran was that he must resist the force of occupation for years—for generations even—if it threatened the faith and his way of life. He paused . . . "We've watched you for 3½ years. We've discussed this in Syria, in Saudi, in Jordan, and in Iraq. And we have come to the conclusion that you do not threaten our way of life. Al Qaeda does."*
> (Gen. Stanley McChrystal, My Share of the Task, p. 248)

Similar turning points were reached all over the battlefield. There was a fairly reliable template: Anbar started turning around in September 2007 (the start of the Awakening plus additional Marines and Army troops and expanded operations) but the violence didn't subside until the following spring. The Awakening then expanded, but it wasn't easy to see. Indeed, the overall level of violence didn't noticeably decline until the fall of 2008 as Baghdad, Diyala, Salahaddin, and other cities were subjected to large-scale Multi-National Force-Iraq Coalition operations and supported by tribal forces.

The Iraqi Awakening—and similar successes in Afghanistan—might have gone even faster, and proven more durable, if we had more aggressively challenged the doctrines of al Qaeda and the Taliban. There were numerous Iraqi imams who rejected the revolutionary doctrines of the insurgents. Chief among them was the most important Shi'ite religious figure, Grand Ayatollah Ali al-Sistani. Sistani exemplified the "moderate" Muslim. From the earliest days following the invasion, he ceaselessly counseled cooperation between Shi'ites and Sunnis, even calling for calm and understanding after the bloodiest sectarian attacks. His was the strongest and most revered voice in the Iraqi Shi'ite community, and we should have echoed it. In like manner, we should have denounced the Islamists' embrace of suicide terrorism and their constant efforts to provoke a sectarian civil war.

This did not happen in either Iraq or Afghanistan, nor is it happening today anywhere in the Middle East. It should. There are plenty of Islamic religious leaders who, like Sistani, detest the radical jihadis. Yet senior American policymakers, ever since 9/11, have shied away from any criticism of Islam, repeating, despite all manner of evidence to the contrary, that "Islam is a religion of peace." This insistence on denying the existence of jihad led President Obama to the absurd claim that the Islamic State has nothing to do with Islam.

We're not going to win this war by denying what's in front of our collective nose. It's long past time for us to denounce the many evils of Radical Islam. The people in the region know it well, as anybody could see by looking at the millions of Iraqis and Afghans who risked their lives to vote in their respective elections despite the jihadis' promise to kill them.

Despite our failure to attack our enemies' ideology, we still defeated them every time we went after them on the battlefield. Their successes invariably came hard on the heels of our decisions to withdraw, first in Iraq and then in Afghanistan. It's difficult to find anyone who thinks that the Surge in Afghanistan achieved anything remotely approaching that in Iraq, but I disagree.

It wasn't easy, and Afghanistan was tougher than Iraq.

When we arrived in Afghanistan in June 2009 we found an HQ in complete disarray, while the enemy was on the march. The threats were increasing and expanding around the country and we felt the International HQ was under siege. Few of the international officers had even left the HQ to travel outside the compound. And the military systems and processes you would expect to find in order to understand what was going on around the battlefield, especially after eight years, weren't in place. Frankly, it was disappointing, and after so many years, we suddenly found ourselves starting from scratch—again.

Upon assuming command, General McChrystal immediately started to tighten everything up. He instilled a sense of discipline into the staff and into the leadership around the country as quickly as he could. Many of the first steps he took were neither welcomed by the international team nor by some on the American side. One of the seemingly minor things was shutting down the alcohol-serving bar inside of the ISAF compound. Here we were in a Muslim country in the middle of a war and the International HQ was holding drinking parties practically every night. Officers, enlisted, civilians, you name it, were carrying on and making all sorts of noise. You could hear all of this in the relatively quiet city of Kabul and everyone knew. The Afghans didn't like it at all. We weren't seen as serious, about them or ourselves. This type of behavior certainly didn't carry that message. The same lack of serious commitment existed all over the battlefield at every major HQ as well as at some of the camps down to at least brigade level. There was too much of an attitude that we're here to simply participate, get a combat patch, and return home. Instead of merely participating in this war, we needed to instill an attitude that we needed to win.

This had to stop. We had to get the U.S. forces and the international team back on track and fast. At least that is what we thought we needed.

However, like all wars, you can never discount your enemy and one of the welcoming messages from the Taliban was a massive vehicle-borne improvised explosive bomb (VBIED) delivered to the front entrance of ISAF HQ early one morning. This came only a few days after General McChrystal had assumed command. It was the Taliban's way of saying, Welcome to Afghanistan.

The attack happened in the middle of our early-morning battlefield update. It was so large, so explosive, that it shook the entire compound. The explosion seemed to lift the building we were occupying. Everyone started to run outside when General McChrystal very calmly directed everyone to stop and get back into their seats and focus on what we had to do—fight and win this war. He was right. And at that moment, at least those in the HQ knew that McChrystal was deadly serious and that a laser focus on winning was now going to be the norm. There would be little time to worry about all the nonsense we found upon first arrival to Kabul. Things had to change and change fast—we were losing.

All of this took place in the first couple of weeks.

After these initial days, some discipline returned to the HQ, and Stan and I and other staff conducted a "listening tour" around the entire country. The results were ugly: we knew very little about the population we were here to supposedly protect, and we were alarmingly ignorant about the strength of al Qaeda and the Taliban. This tour was a descent into some of the most notorious places in Afghanistan, but it was indispensable. We met with our commanders and their staffs at their various operational HQs (down to platoon and squad level), but more important, we met with Afghans. We went into remote and rural villages and cities, we met with local tribal leaders and provincial governors. We met with police officers and many in the Afghan military. There were battlefield updates from our forces about how well we were doing (most all of it subsequently demonstrated to have been BS) and numerous but mostly whispered complaints about the extraordinary level of corruption rampant inside the entire ecosystem—including our own people.

As is often the case, the most accurate information came from the lower levels of our fighters. They did not bullshit us. They didn't have time to waste our time for any nonsense, nor did they have the resources from the policymakers they badly needed. They also didn't know many of the basic things they needed to know if we were going to prevail; they lacked any real intelligence other than what they discovered on the terrain they were operating on. I felt bad. I had come from the world of special operations where we brought intelligence to the forefront of our operations. We had changed the mentality from fighting a plan to fighting our enemy—we had operationalized intelligence and we did so for our most elite military forces. I was proud of that, but I saw in our conventional forces a complete lack of real intelligence support.

All the baloney you hear about "national to tactical" is crap. Here we were in the first decade of the twenty-first century and despite advances in technology, our conventional military forces fighting at the edge of the battlefield were very limited in their vision and understanding of the battlefield. There was simply no good technology down to the local level enabling them to "see" the enemy the way higher headquarters were able to see them. There was a need to change what we were providing our troops at the edge and we proceeded to do that. In the meantime, thank God they were so brave, ingenious in how they executed their mission, extremely well trained, and innovative. There is something about the American soldier—despite our best efforts to shit on them, they rise to the occasion and perform miraculously.

Before going back to Afghanistan in June 2009, I had most recently served at Central Command and for the chairman of the Joint Chiefs in the Pentagon, pristine areas where you get all the intelligence you want and on a constant basis. The problem is, that intelligence doesn't do you a bit of good if you aren't able to get it to those who can actually do something about it. And in those assignments, I found that "intelligence," the really sensitive stuff, was routinely outdated and therefore irrelevant. I was quickly starting to see that the world of open source information from media on the battlefield was becoming more and more useful—this would pay off later on with the rapid rise of social media.

During this listening tour, many soldiers and civilians we spoke to complained about the disconnect between the government of Hamid Karzai, the international community, our military forces, and the rest of the country. Nearly everywhere we traveled, whether by helicopter, foot, or vehicle, there was this incredible loss of confidence stated by everyone. They lacked confidence in us, and they especially had zero confidence in their own government.

Our investigation took us into early July, but it was only a first take. I needed to know a lot more. It was clear that the intelligence system was badly broken. There was nothing remotely approaching what we'd created in Iraq. There were few resources and an almost complete disconnect from what our men and women saw on the ground to what we were reporting up to our higher HQ. Overall, the Taliban had returned, al Qaeda was back (and stronger than before) and were now in possession of large swaths of Afghanistan. Even though the president of the United States said that Afghanistan was his main priority, the Pentagon and the rest of the system, the intelligence community included, simply could not and did not adjust. The focus was still on Iraq.

In mid-July 2009, I took a small team back around the country examining the intelligence operations in a far more detailed way. Speaking to many of the Afghan people as far down into the various villages as we could go was essential. I also started to develop relationships during this period with some very notorious characters. One was Colonel (now General) Abdul Razziq of Spin Boldak in southern Kandahar Province, another was Ahmed Wali Karzai (AWK), half brother to President Karzai.

They weren't Boy Scouts. Razziq was known for his

narcotics and poppy smuggling down across the Pakistan border at a place called Friendship Gate—though there were no friends nor anything friendly coming across that gate. He was a slim, wiry, and extremely tough guy. He showed me a couple of bullet wounds he had taken fighting the Taliban. Most Americans likely only see such a person in *National Geographic*. The Taliban had killed at least two of his brothers and had tried to kill him on more than one occasion. Despite his many unsavory characteristics, I liked Razziq; he was straightforward with me, as I was with him. We actually got along with each other and this paid off down the road. It was the first time anyone from the ISAF level or even the government had paid any attention to him and he was in charge of a large portion of an extremely important and very dangerous piece of geography, southern Kandahar. It was the gateway to Pakistan's southern border region and directly across the border from the Taliban's HQ in a notorious place called Quetta.

I didn't like what he represented nor what he did, but we needed him badly. He maintained stability in his tribal areas, he knew what was needed, and he ruled with an iron fist. He also knew things our troops desperately had to know. I traveled with him in a beat-up Toyota truck one day through his turf. As we drove through some villages, he would veer off the road and along what can only be described as a path that, he knew, was clear of mines and other explosives. Men and young children (girls and boys) would come up to him and he would hand out Afghan money. I felt like I was with someone out of a Robin Hood story. They loved him.

He showed me that the human terrain in Afghanistan and the fabric of the society were vastly different from Iraq and we could not impose similar actions on this environment, as we had in Iraq. Getting tribal leaders to come over to our side was going to be very difficult and if we were going to use this type of approach, we would have to work just as hard in multiple areas of the country, and with multiple tribal leaders—there would be no Anbar Awakening in Afghanistan as a whole. We were going to have to do it piece by piece. It would take far more time and more resources, but I strongly believed we could prevail.

From an intelligence perspective, we needed a far more granular sense of the ground. We were in a race for knowledge and we were losing. Through Razziq, I met other Afghans and because I treated him with respect, when I met with others, I got respect back—I needed it in some of the places I ended up going into.

I took Razziq along with Lieutenant General Mohammad Noorzai (commander of the Afghan Border Police) for a visit to the Torkham Gate in the east, as well as up to one of the northern border crossings, to show him what we needed him to do at the Friendship Gate and throughout the challenging southern part of Afghanistan. This trip was an eye-opener for him and me. It was the first time Razziq had ever been in a plane (at first he thought I was there to have him arrested). The objectives of this trip were to develop a stronger relationship with someone we needed on our side, and to show Razziq what a more organized border crossing looked like. The former was what I was looking for in this trip; to achieve the latter at Friendship Gate in southern Kandahar would eventually take well over a year to even get started.

Razziq's suspicions about me potentially arresting him weren't just paranoia. We had arrested Razziq's fellow provincial border chief of police in Helmand, the guy who ran the infamous Pakistan border town of Baramshah. Baramshah was a lot like Tombstone in the Wild West movies, but on poppy-filled steroids. There were all sorts of nefarious activities in and around that town. One of the things the Helmand chief of police did that government officials were willing to arrest him for, was steal money from families of Afghan soldiers. He was essentially collecting money from the families of his dead police officers. The government was still paying for them and he was reporting they were still alive. I found this practice to be rampant around the country—this may still be the case, although we tried to stop it—but at the time, there was no system in place to correct this behavior other than to stop paying the entire police force. Looking back, we probably should have taken that extreme measure to send a message that we were serious about corruption.

The minister of the interior, Hanif Atmar (a man trained

by the Soviets), agreed with our plan to have one of his "leaders" arrested. It was a pretty dramatic operation. We flew a plane down to Kandahar airfield, deceived the police chief into thinking he was attending a meeting with his leadership at the airfield, and upon his arrival had him arrested. He was placed on the aircraft, brought back to Kabul where he faced a kangaroo court–type hearing that summarily removed him from his position and subsequently released him back out into the wild. He returned to Helmand Province in a new role, as a fighter in the ranks of the Taliban! You cannot make this stuff up.

By 2011, the Marines had largely succeeded at their intended task of subduing Helmand, and the Army had achieved similar results in Kandahar. Given that severely under-resourced U.K. forces had been fighting from 2006 to 2010 without relief, that's a pretty impressive accomplishment. In 2013 there was a widespread grassroots tribal rebellion among several of the senior Pashtun tribes that could have provided us with an Awakening-like opportunity, but alas it wasn't supported by the Karzai government or resourced by the international community. The predictable, heartbreaking result was that everyone who trusted us was abandoned to the tender mercies of the terrorists—similar to what occurred in Iraq.

Subsequently, the Taliban and its allies have regained their lost territory. The problem is that because those strategic opportunities weren't understood at the time (much like the assessment of Anbar in Iraq on the eve of the Awakening), hardly anyone recognizes just how close we actually came to winning in Afghanistan. But then, as in Iraq, winning isn't going to be durable if your next move is retreat.

As in Iraq, I worked alongside General McChrystal, and as in Iraq, it was necessary to totally revamp both the way we did intelligence and the relationship between intel and operations.

3

The Enemy Alliance

Democracy's greatest weakness is foreign policy, as Alexis de Tocqueville wrote way back in 1831. We are slow, and we can't keep secrets very well, whereas an effective national security policy often requires secrecy and high speed, lest our enemies get even stronger and are justifiably confident that they know what we will and won't do.

Therefore, it is often impossible for democratic leaders—even if they do see what is happening and have enough vision and courage to respond—to take properly prudent and timely action before the full onset of a major crisis.

Winston Churchill, one of the few British leaders to see the Nazi threat early and fully, was widely ridiculed until the Second World War was already under way. In America, months before we were attacked at Pearl Harbor on December 7, 1941, it took all the political skills of Franklin Delano Roosevelt to gain congressional approval for the military draft, by a single vote, in August 1941.

The slogans of political correctness have reinforced these weaknesses. If, as PC apologists tell us, there is no objective basis for members of one culture to criticize another, then it is very hard to see—and forbidden to write about or say—the existence of an international alliance of evil countries and movements that is working to destroy us.

Yet, the alliance exists, and we've already dithered for many years.

The war is on. We face a working coalition that extends from North Korea and China to Russia, Iran, Syria, Cuba, Bolivia, Venezuela, and Nicaragua. We are under attack, not only from nation-states directly, but also from al Qaeda, Hezbollah, ISIS, and countless other terrorist groups. (I will discuss later on, the close working relationships between terror groups and organized criminal organizations.) Suffice to say, the same sort of cooperation binds together jihadis, Communists, and garden-variety tyrants.

This alliance surprises a lot of people. On the surface, it seems incoherent. How, they ask, can a Communist regime like North Korea embrace a radical Islamist regime like Iran? What about Russia's Vladimir Putin? He is certainly no jihadi; indeed, Russia has a good deal to fear from radical Islamist groups to its south, and the Russians have been very heavy-handed with Radical Islamists in places like Chechnya.

Yet the Russian air force and Iranian foot soldiers are fighting side by side in Syria.

Somehow, Russian antipathy toward radical Islam does not prevent the Kremlin from constructing all the Iranian nuclear power plants, nor does the doctrinaire Communist regime in Pyongyang hesitate to cooperate with Tehran regarding nuclear weapons, missiles, petroleum, and tunnels.

Iran is the linchpin of the alliance, its centerpiece.

The Pyongyang-Tehran partnership is quite long-standing and extensive:

> *Both Iran and North Korea were part of the A. Q. Khan (nuclear weapons) proliferation network, and bilateral trade in oil and weapons has continued despite UN resolutions designed to stop it. Ballistic missile cooperation is documented, and nuclear cooperation has been an unspoken theme in Washington. Pyongyang helped Damascus, Iran's ally, build a secret reactor. There are reports that North Korean experts visited Iran in May [2015] to help Iran with its missile program. Pressed by reporters on the subject of North Korea–Iran nuclear cooperation a few weeks ago, even the State Department acknowledged that it takes reports of such cooperation seriously.* (www.jewishpolicycenter .org/5643/does-iran-already-have-nuclear-weapons)

There is a considerable volume of air traffic between the two countries, and the North Koreans have long assisted the

Iranians in digging tunnels. More important, in early September 2007, Israeli forces allegedly destroyed a potential nuclear weapons site in Syria that was under Iranian operation and had benefited from North Korean technological assistance.

At the time, I was the senior intelligence officer at the United States Central Command. We spent many sleepless nights planning a series of operations to strike these facilities. The more I studied the extensive construction, the number of sites, the connections between North Korea and Iran as well as the operations security that kept these facilities hidden for nearly ten years right under our noses, I grew more irritated and angry than being simply disappointed in our intelligence system. Missing this site was beyond being an intelligence failure, it could have caused a nuclear war in the Middle East.

And according to the German press at the time—*Der Spiegel*—there were at least two other nuclear weapons facilities in Syria as a result of Iranian–North Korean efforts. One was an underground location near the Lebanese border. The other was said to be at a "secret location." In the end, we were lucky the Israelis decided to attack and destroy Al-Kibar—today, ISIS owns that territory and would likely own a nuclear weapon.

Iran

If you go to the official Web site of the Iranian supreme leader, Ali Khameini, you will find him described as "the leader of the Muslims," endowed with the authority of the ancient caliphs to lead all Muslims, not just the Shi'ites.

Ayatollah Ruhollah Khomeini's revolution in early 1979 toppled not only the shah, but traditional Shi'ite doctrine, according to which civil society must not be governed by clerics until the return of the "Vanished Imam," whose reappearance would usher in the millennium. In contrast with Sunni doctrine, the Shi'ites had long insisted that the mosque was the rightful place for religious leaders, leaving government to secular power. Khomeini himself assumed power in Iran, and put in place a stern, oppressive system that drove women from public life, enforced puritanical regulations on the population, and carried out mass executions of those who challenged him.

It was, and remains, a classic example of clerical fascism. Like the leaders of other fascist states, the mullahs who have ruled the Islamic Republic have claimed universal authority in the name of their doctrine, not of their country. And they say they are prepared to die—along with their followers—to accomplish their mission. As Khomeini put it shortly after the occupation of the American embassy in Tehran in 1979: "We do not worship Iran, we worship Allah. . . . For patriotism is another name for paganism. I say let this land burn. I say let this land go up in smoke, provided Islam emerges triumphant in the rest of the world."

Khomeini and his successors have been true to their words, seeking to export the Iranian Revolution, and attack their enemies—the Jews, the infidels, and (mostly Sunni) Muslims who do not accept their doctrine—all over the world. Shortly after the revolution, Iranian-supported "pilgrims" on the Hajj in Mecca occupied the Grand Mosque, took several hundred hostages, and called for the overthrow of the ruling Saudi royal family, and the end of all ties to the West. The Grand Mosque became a battleground, and it took two weeks of tough fighting—and some 250 dead, including scores of Saudi national guardsmen, and hundreds wounded—to reestablish order.

The assault on the Grand Mosque had a significant footnote: the first appearance of the name bin Laden in conjunction with a terrorist attack. Osama bin Laden's brother Mahrous was apparently involved in the operation, and was miraculously spared the executioner's scimitar. He even gained early release from prison, abandoned political activism, and subsequently devoted all his energies to the family business.

Ever since, Iran has sponsored terrorism all over the world, and has ceaselessly attacked the United States in word and deed. For many years, the State Department has declared the Islamic Republic the leading supporter of international, state-sponsored terrorism, and for good reason. The Iranians created

the Islamic Jihad organization, and Hezbollah, the big terrorist army based in Lebanon and now Syria. Moreover, Iran has
long supported al Qaeda, which baffles a lot of people because
it is a Sunni organization. The explanation is quite simple:
like Mafia families who fight and sometimes kill one another,
when faced with a common enemy, the family heads sit
down around the table and make a common war plan. The
ties between the Iranian regime and al Qaeda have been a
well-established fact ever since the autumn of 1998, when the
American government indicted the organization and its leader,
Osama bin Laden. The key section of the indictment states
the case explicitly: "Al Qaeda forged alliances with the National
Islamic Front in the Sudan and with the government of Iran
and its associated terrorist group, Hezbollah, for the purpose
of working together against their perceived common enemies
in the West, particularly the United States."

By the time this indictment was issued, we knew that al
Qaeda had attacked us directly, in 1993, in the first attempt to
bring down the World Trade Center in New York City. Federal
investigators had established working connections between
al Qaeda and the commander of the operation, the "blind
sheikh" Omar Abdel-Rahman. We also knew of close operational cooperation with the Muslim Brotherhood, the Egyptian jihadi organization that had been at the center of the
assassination of President Anwar al-Sadat.

As a matter of fact, the Iranian Revolutionary Guards,

which were originally created by Khomeini as his own personal praetorian guard, and subsequently used for crucial tasks of domestic repression and foreign terrorism, were trained and organized in the early 1970s by Yasser Arafat's (Sunni) Fatah.

The most dramatic example of Sunni-Shi'ite cooperation is Iran's close relationship with Osama bin Laden's al Qaeda. The 1998 embassy bombings in East Africa—for which al Qaeda took credit—were in large part Iranian operations. Bin Laden had asked Hezbollah's operational chief, Imad Mughniyah (one of the most dangerous terrorists to ever walk the earth), for help making al Qaeda as potent as Hezbollah, and the original concept for the simultaneous bombings in Kenya and Tanzania came directly from Mughniyah.

The al Qaeda terrorists were trained by Hezbollah in Lebanon, and the explosives were provided by Iran. After the attacks, one of the leaders of the operations, Saif al-Adel, took refuge in Iran, where he remains active in operations as of this writing.

Abu Musab al-Zarqawi, the Sunni leader of al Qaeda in Iraq, which evolved into today's Islamic State, created his first international terror network while based in Iran, as demonstrated by court documents in Germany and Italy from the late 1990s. The public record of the trials contains hundreds of intercepts of conversations between Zarqawi in Tehran and the terrorists in Europe.

Anyone who believes that the Iranian regime was unaware of Zarqawi's activities doesn't understand the way Iran works.

The principal instrument of Iranian terror is often Hezbollah, which was created in Lebanon (where the Syrians provided safe haven) shortly after the revolution. In the 1980s, Hezbollah—operating in tandem with the Palestine Liberation Organization (PLO)—organized suicide bombing attacks against the French and American Marine barracks, and the American embassy in Beirut, as well as the kidnappings of American missionaries and military and intelligence officers, who were then tortured to death. In the 1990s, Hezbollah conducted lethal attacks against Jewish targets in Argentina, for which leaders of the Iranian regime have been indicted. Of late, the Iranians have also used their "foreign legion" (Quds Force) of the Revolutionary Guards, especially in the bloody fighting in Syria.

An American federal judge has ruled that Iran was responsible for the 1996 Khobar Towers bombing in Saudi Arabia, in which nineteen American Air Force personnel were killed and 372 wounded. The ruling was based in large part on sworn testimony from former FBI director Louis Freeh, who had investigated the bombings at the time they took place. He found that two Iranian government security agencies and senior members of the Iranian government (including Khamenei and intelligence chief Ali Fallahian) provided funding, training, and explosives and logistical assistance to the terrorists (who referred to themselves as "Saudi Hezbollah," thereby explicitly confirming their ties to the mullahs).

Iranian cooperation with al Qaeda is not just a recent development, nor is it limited to the Middle East. In February 1996, British NATO forces in Bosnia found a manual for training terrorists that a British expert called "the mother of all training manuals." It was uncovered during an operation against a terrorist training camp in Pogorelica, during which Bosnian police arrested four Iranian "diplomats" and eight Bosnian Muslims. The manual had been produced by the Iranian Intelligence Ministry, and had been earlier used to train al Qaeda militants in Sudan. It was a thoroughly professional job, and included sections ranging from clandestine communications, to the creation of a secure terrorist cell (including recruitment and maintenance of good morale), to staging simultaneous attacks, kidnapping, evading surveillance, and discourses on the anti-Western jihad.

The considerable sophistication of the training manual greatly surprised the British analysts, as it would the Americans with whom it was shared six years later, in 2002. The surprise was at a piece of equipment that subsequently astonished the Israelis during their war with Hezbollah in the summer of 2006. The Israel Defense Forces discovered that the terrorists were using highly advanced electronic surveillance devices, provided by the Iranian Revolutionary Guards, at a cost of tens of millions of dollars. During the conflict, Hezbollah used two new listening stations to monitor Israeli communications, one in the Golan Heights and the other at Baab al-Hawa, near the Turkish border. (www.jewishpolicycenter.org/20/the-iranian-time -bomb)

When we found the Iranians on the Iraqi and Afghan battlefields, we told the policymakers, hoping to get the green light to go after them. Instead, two consecutive administrations didn't want to hear about it. By the end of the Bush administration, our military commanders in Afghanistan and Iraq had become very outspoken about the Iranian role.

Referring to the new generation of roadside bombs (EFPs or explosively formed projectiles), and the discovery of substantial shipments of weapons, ammunition, and explosives, Army General Dan McNeill, who commanded 40,000 troops in the International Security Assistance Force in Afghanistan, the ISAF, said in the autumn of 2007, "this weapons convoy clearly, geographically, originated in Iran. It is difficult for me to conceive that this . . . could have originated in Iran and come to Afghanistan, without at least the knowledge of the Iranian military." At the same time a British spokesman in Kabul said, "this confirms our view that elements within Iran are supporting the Sunni Taliban."

In Iraq, U.S. Major General William Caldwell said "it's not all Sunni insurgents but . . . we do know is that there is a direct awareness by Iranian intelligence officials that they are providing support to some selective Sunni insurgent elements."

And General David Petraeus announced that the Iranians were "funding, over the last several years, certainly hundreds of millions of dollars of assistance to different Shia militia groups, and we have found evidence very recently of assistance being provided to Sunni Arab groups as well. One of the Sunni insurgent leaders was just over in Tehran."

Our military leaders (including myself) stressed, as we would later on, that the proof of Iranian involvement sometimes came directly from the terrorists themselves. Here's General Caldwell again: "Detainees in American custody have indicated that Iranian intelligence operatives have given support to Sunni insurgents, and then we've discovered some munitions in Baghdad neighborhoods which are largely Sunni that were manufactured in Iran." In addition, General Caldwell told reporters that we knew of radical Iraqi Shi'ites being trained in Iran.

The Iranians have few peers when it comes to killing—in 2015, Iran had the highest per capita execution rate in the world, and in total numbers was second only to the People's Republic of China—and they excel at deception, as witness their secret nuclear program.

They are a formidable enemy, and they have been at war with the United States, its friends, and its allies (notably Israel) for nearly forty years. Tehran's war against the West is not based on a desire for territory, or on real or imagined grievances; it is rooted in the nature of the Islamic Republic, and it rests on ultimate issues. For the Iranians to negotiate a modus vivendi with us would be tantamount to abandoning the messianic vision of Khomeini and his successors.

The wars in Iraq and Afghanistan, which so many take as the starting point for their analysis of Iran's behavior, is only one chapter in the story of the Iranian war against the West; Iraq is one more battlefield on which the Iranians have killed Western soldiers and civilians. Only the scale is new; the practice was already well established long before Operation Iraqi Freedom was even conceived. In many respects, the Iranian/ Syrian strategy in Iraq after our invasion of 2004 was little more than a replay of the successful methods used against us in Lebanon in the 1980s: suicide terrorism, hostage taking, mass demonstrations, and manipulation of the media. This strategy was announced publicly by Bashar al-Assad in a published interview, before we ever set one boot in Iraq. Nonetheless, the violence of the Iranian response, in tandem with their Syrian allies, surprised most Western strategists. They should not have been surprised, since the pattern was established in 1979 and has been followed ever since.

Once we bailed out of Iraq in 2011, the power of the Islamic Republic immediately expanded and rapidly filled the void left by our departure. The mullahs have already established strategic alliances in our own hemisphere with Cuba and Venezuela, and are working closely with Russia and China; a victory over the "Great Satan" in Iraq will compel the smaller Middle

Eastern countries to come to terms with Tehran, and make the region much more inhospitable to us and our friends and allies. All of this can be accomplished without atomic bombs— the issue that dominates the policy debate over Iran throughout the West.

To be sure, an Iranian bomb would be an existential threat to Israel, but so is a nonnuclear Iran, which is the mainstay of the anti-Israel terrorist groups, above all, Hamas and Islamic Jihad. To focus solely on the nuclear question is a serious failure of strategic vision; the issue is the regime in Tehran and their radical version of Islam, whatever its progress may be toward atomic bombs.

Nor does Iran need atomic bombs to gravely threaten American security. Every day we see evidence of Iranian espionage in the United States—to take the most recent example, a man named Mohammed Alavi was arrested for providing Iran with the floor plan of America's largest nuclear power plant—and numerous Iranian "diplomats" at the United Nations have been thrown out of New York City when they were found taking photographs of train and subway stations. It is hard to imagine that there are no Hezbollah terrorist groups inside this country. If they could blow up buildings in Buenos Aires, they can surely do the same here, and they have bragged that they have studied our weak points carefully, and are ready to attack when circumstances are more favorable.

Unfortunately, for nearly forty years every American

administration has permitted the Islamic Republic to build up its strength, and even organize assassinations in our capital. Jimmy Carter, Bill Clinton, and Ronald Reagan either directly sold weapons to Iran, or enabled others to do it, as in the case of the secret Gore-Chernomyrdin deal (in violation of then-Senator Al Gore's own legislation). In all those years, no American president has initiated a serious challenge to post-revolutionary Iran, a pattern that now extends to our inconclusive response to the Islamic State. Indeed, the only time Iran paid a price for attacking American targets was when an American naval vessel hit an Iranian mine in the Persian Gulf during the Reagan presidency. When we responded by attacking Iranian targets in the area, the Iranian navy escalated the confrontation, and suffered the loss of about one third of their ships. But no American president has called for regime change in Tehran; no American administration has supported the many millions of Iranian dissidents, including workers, teachers, students, and others who have demonstrated a desire for democracy and the courage to fight for it. Indeed, our Persian-language radio and television broadcasting to Iran more often than not has been more critical of the United States than of the clerical fascists who threaten us. Our feeble response to the global war against us is reminiscent of the first years of Jimmy Carter.

President Obama's Cairo speech was in many ways a throwback to Carter's famous "we have outgrown our inordinate fear of Communism" pronouncement that he delivered at Notre Dame. History reminds us that President Carter, in essence, said that the Soviet Union and international Communism were really nothing to worry about, that the Cold War was over, and that we would henceforth conduct a suitably modest foreign policy instead of the strident, aggressive, morally improper kind that his predecessors had waged. We would support human rights everywhere, but not in such a way as to threaten hostile tyrants.

Thereafter, throughout what used to be known as the Third World, Carter not only abandoned several friendly tyrants (the most famous was the shah of Iran) to insurrections organized by our enemies, but piously acted as if we couldn't do anything about it anyway, nor should we wish to do so. After all, we had sinned by supporting those tyrants, and it was only right for them to be overthrown.

In like manner, in today's Third World, Obama has shown great sympathy for anti-American "revolutionaries," and abandoned friendly tyrannies such as Hosni Mubarak's Egypt and Zine Ben Ali's Tunisia. And just as Carter was reluctant to challenge Communist control in the Soviet Union, Cuba, and Nicaragua, so Obama has been reluctant to support the domestic opponents of Islamist regimes in Damascus and Tehran. One of the best short summaries of the dangerous foolishness of Obama's foreign policy goes like this:

Inconsistencies are a familiar part of politics in most societies. Usually, however, governments behave hypocritically when their principles conflict with the national interest. What makes the inconsistencies of the Obama administration noteworthy are, first, the administration's moralism, which renders it especially vulnerable to charges of hypocrisy; and, second, the administration's predilection for policies that violate the strategic and economic interests of the United States. The administration's conception of national interest borders on doublethink: it finds friendly powers to be guilty representatives of the status quo and views the triumph of unfriendly groups as beneficial to America's "true interests."

I have made one change in the original text above. I inserted "Obama" in place of "Carter." The paragraph comes from Ambassador Jeane Kirkpatrick's essay "Dictatorships and Double Standards," which appeared in *Commentary* magazine in November 1979. The name change demonstrates how the two worst presidents we've ever elected act so similarly.

Ambassador Kirkpatrick's critique of Carter applies in equal measure to Obama. Like Carter, President Obama is vulnerable to charges of hypocrisy (if it was right to intervene in Libya, why not in Syria and Iran, two regimes that kill Americans in addition to slaughtering their own?), and there is an additional convergence: both American presidents have instinctive sympathy, even enthusiasm, for self-proclaimed anti-American "revolutionaries." Here's Ambassador Kirkpatrick again:

> *A posture of continuous self-abasement and apology vis-a-vis the Third World is neither morally necessary nor politically appropriate. No more is it necessary or appropriate to support vocal enemies of the United States because they invoke the rhetoric of popular liberation. . . . Liberal idealism need not be identical with masochism, and need not be incompatible with the defense of freedom and the national interest.*

Indeed, if you're really interested in advancing freedom (which I fervently believe is in our American national interest), you should fight against our vocal enemies. They invariably turn out to be real enemies and will translate their words into terrorists, guns, and weapons of mass destruction as soon as they have a chance. Obama has done his damnedest to forge alliances with Hugo Chavez, before his death, the Castro brothers, and Ali Khamenei, but they and their cronies have all responded by redoubling their efforts to defeat us.

Both presidents displayed a curious sympathy with our enemies. Carter told the dictator of Poland that he had not given up on bringing the Communist "back to Christianity," and Obama has striven mightily to cut deals with the Iranians,

Cubans, and other Latin American radicals who have joined the enemy alliance.

As with twentieth-century Fascist and Communist totalitarian regimes, the current crop of Islamist and secular totalitarian regimes in the Middle East say what they mean, and act on it.

What works? Ironically, Ronald Reagan proved to be the true revolutionary. While liberals like Carter invited the success of radicals who installed totalitarian regimes, Reagan supported democratic forces in both friendly and unfriendly tyrannies, from the Soviet Union to Argentina. Reagan knew what both Carter and now Obama reject: that America is the one truly revolutionary country in the world, and part of our national mission is to support democratic revolutionaries against their oppressors.

Late in the third year of his presidency, Jimmy Carter had an epiphany when the Soviets invaded Afghanistan. At which point, fear of Communism was no longer irrational in his eyes. He began the expansion of our military budget that ultimately made the United States so powerful that the gray men in the Kremlin did not dare to lash out at us when the bell tolled for the Soviet Empire.

Obama (and our country) is now at a similar historic juncture. Does he now see the urgency of responding to the anti-American tyrants in Cuba, Venezuela, Iran, and Syria? Will he support their opponents? Will he ever come to grips with the likes of Radical Islamism and its allies? Not bloody likely!

Secular Radicals, Jihadi Radicals

On the face of it, the alliance between Russia and Iran is surprising. No doubt Vladimir Putin remembers that the Ayatollah Khomeini called upon Soviet dictator Leonid Brezhnev to convert to Islam, and Putin knows well that the Iranians sent thousands of Korans and many radical imams into the Muslim regions of the USSR. Putin himself waged a bloody battle against Radical Islamists in Chechnya, and they, too, had links to Iran.

It seems very unlikely that Putin is pleased by the thought of a fanatical Muslim state virtually on his borders. One of the wisest analysts of Putin's thinking, Walter Laqueur, notes in his book *Putinism* that "it is difficult to assess the prospects of the militant Islamic movement, because most of their activities take place underground. It seems probable that at least some of the militants of the Afghan war will invade the Central Asian republics." He adds that Putin is reluctant (to fully integrate countries like) Tajikistan and Kyrgyzstan into the Russian Federation, preferring governments with limited independence. Laqueur judges it is likely that "parts of Central Asia will remain danger zones." These are areas where the Iranians have been actively sponsoring Shi'ite radicalism.

These are very serious concerns, yet Putin has done a lot for the Khamenei regime. Russian involvement in Persian affairs goes back centuries, and I have pointed out that there are very close working relations between the two countries, the most spectacular example being the Iranian nuclear program. The nuclear reactor at Bushehr is a Russian product, as will be the next two reactors. Iran has contracted for billions of dollars' worth of military equipment, as well as very good Russian antiaircraft missiles, the infamous S–300s. Finally, there is no denying the fact that the two are fighting side by side in Syria trying to save the regime of their mutual ally, Bashar al-Assad.

How does one explain this superficially unlikely partnership? In part, it's the old nostrum: "The enemy of my enemy is my friend." Putin has declared the United States (and NATO generally) to be a national security threat to Russia, and "Death to America" is the official chant of the Islamic Republic of Iran. Both the Putinists and the radical Iranian Muslims agree on the identity of their main enemy. Hence, one part of the answer is surely that their alliance is simply the logical outgrowth of their hostility toward America. Certainly it would be a mistake to describe the relationship as a warm embrace; there is precious little trust between the two, and if they fail to win in Syria, we can expect to hear some very nasty rhetoric coming out of Moscow and Tehran.

Is this, then, simply an alliance of convenience? Is it to be explained by one of the hard rules of geopolitics—the existence of a common enemy? And does this account for the global alliance, from Pyongyang to Havana? What about the presence of ISIS and al Qaeda in the alliance? I don't believe it is.

The Russians and Iranians have more in common than a shared enemy. There is also a shared contempt for democracy and an agreement—by all the members of the enemy alliance—that dictatorship is a superior way to run a country, an empire, or a caliphate. There are certainly differences between the religious and secular tyrannies—the importance of Sharia law to the jihadis is perhaps the most significant—but both seek, and fight for, an all-powerful leader.

Recent public opinion polls in Russia show that the great majority of young people believe "there was a national leader deciding all important political issues concerning the presence in the future of their country; the rest of the people had no influence on this, and there was no reason to change this state of affairs." The dividing line between religious and secular tyranny is often fuzzy, and, except for the Communist regimes in North Korea and Cuba, none of our enemies accepts the notion of separation of church (or mosque) and state. The Russian Orthodox Church is now far more powerful than it was during the Communist years, and, contrary to conventional wisdom, Radical Islam played a major role in Saddam Hussein's Iraq long before our arrival in 2003.

Religious convictions are far more potent in recruiting

followers, whether by mass movements or nominally secular regimes, than intellectual tracts or legalistic documents. Religion provides believers with the meaning of life; even the mightiest of dictators can't do that. This is nowhere better demonstrated than in the history of the Islamic State, which was spawned by Saddam Hussein himself.

It was long said that Baathism, the official doctrine of Saddam in Iraq and the Assads in Syria, was an Arab secular socialism. It was proclaimed during the seizure of power in both countries, and was often cited as the ideological basis for their close ties with the Soviet Union. Based as it was on the Soviet model, Baathism was an effective system for tyrannical rule, but it did not inspire the people. During the Iran-Iraq War in the 1980s, the "godless" nature of Saddam's regime was a centerpiece of Iranian propaganda, and it was quite effective. As a result, Saddam made a basic change in his foreign policy in the summer of 1986, when the Iraqi Politburo (Pan-Arab Command) decided to support foreign "religious currents."

This led to Iraqi support for the Muslim Brotherhood in Egypt, for the radical regime of Hassan al-Turabi in Sudan, the Taliban in Afghanistan, and eventually for al Qaeda. Within Iraq, the Baathist regime starting funding (mostly Sunni but sometimes Shi'ite) mosques and imams. When Baath Party founder Michel Aflaq, a Christian atheist, died in 1989, official eulogies claimed he had converted to Islam. In November of that year, the Saddam University for Islamic Studies opened its doors in Baghdad, the Koran had become required reading (even in official party headquarters), and four years later Saddam announced a full-fledged Faith Campaign.

We're talking 1993, ten years before the U.S. invasion. From then on, the ruling Iraqi elite became increasingly Islamized, so that when the insurrection was organized to fight us and our allies, it was largely led by men who had received two kinds of professional and ideological preparation. As officials of the Baathist state—particularly from the intelligence and counterintelligence branches—they had undergone training by the intelligence organizations of the Soviet Empire. Kyle Orton, Middle East analyst and blogger, and others rightly stress that "All of the leaders of ISIS's Military Council, its most important institution, have since 2010 been [former regime officials]." (https://kyleorton1991.wordpress.com/2015/12/12/the-islamic-state-was-coming-without-the-invasion-of-iraq/)

These men had also received religious indoctrination, and, by 2003 the main precursor of ISIS (the small but growing organization led by Zarqawi) had established religious requirements for new members; they had to pass an entrance examination.

Abu Musab al-Zarqawi was the driving force. He arrived in Baghdad in May 2002 with other top al Qaeda figures. He moved around the country, recruiting individuals such as Aleppo-based Abu Muhammad al-Adnani, the Islamic State's powerful official spokesman, and setting up the ratlines through Syria that would bring the foreign fighters to the Islamic State's predecessor (al Qaeda in Iraq). The Assad regime was complicit in Zarqawi's actions at this time, too, not only in forming the networks that brought the foreign fighters to the Islamic State but in the assassination of USAID worker Laurence Foley in Amman, Jordan. In November 2002, Zarqawi again returned to Iraq and took up residence in Ansar al-Islam–controlled territory, an Iranian proxy. Zarqawi and his band of Ansar fighters fled to Iran during the initial stages of the 2003 U.S. invasion. From interrogations conducted during our operations in Iraq, we learned that for a short period in the spring of 2003, Zarqawi was "detained" by Iran and then subsequently released. While there is little information as to why they detained him, one can only speculate that Iran likely worked with and advised Zarqawi on his future plans for taking over Iraq.

In Saddam's case, he had brought thousands of foreign fighters into Iraq, many through state-directed mosques which were connected to international Islamist networks, and these fighters, under the command of the heavily radicalized loyalist militia, the Fedayeen Saddam, were almost the only resistance against the Coalition invasion.

The war in Iraq foreshadowed the alliance against us, and showed that secular and religious forces, movements, and countries could join forces. Notice again, for example, that Zarqawi went from Iraq to Iran at the start of the war, and then returned. There was no love lost between Saddam and the Iranians, and Zarqawi was not an Iraqi instrument by any means, but both regimes helped him.

The interplay between religion and pure power is also on display in some of the captured ISIS documents published in the Western press. German analysts have been struck by the striking similarity between ISIS bureaucracy—especially when it comes to spying on their own residents—and the notorious Stasi system of control in Communist East Germany (Stasi was the intelligence arm of the former East German regime under Soviet Communist dictatorship). No surprise here; since so many of the top officials of the Islamic State came from Saddam's regime (most of whom were trained by Communists), it was only to be expected that their Sharia-based caliphate would resemble the Soviet bloc.

Thus, religious fanatics and secular tyrants work quite well together, transcending even deep ideological divides. The most dramatic example comes from the infamous case of the grand mufti of Jerusalem in the 1930s and 1940s, Amin al-Husseini, and his efforts to forge an operational relationship between Nazi Germany and his own Muslim Brotherhood.

Israeli prime minister Benjamin Netanyahu catalyzed the discussion of the historical origins of contemporary Islamist anti-Semitism in European Nazi and fascist regimes in the last century, which has produced some useful and thoughtful contributions, but in the process an important part of the story has gone lost. It's the part of the story that deals with Husseini's ties to Soviet Communism. Lenin and Stalin have somehow failed to claim their rightful places at the top of the pedestal of evil; Hitler's got it all to himself. But in the case of Husseini, and indeed of jihadism more generally, any serious discussion must make room for the Communists. Listen to the late scholar Laurent Murawiec in his masterpiece *The Mind of Jihad*:

> *Starting in the 1920s and 1930s the Communist Party of Palestine (CPP) was the great instructor of the pan-Islamist nationalist movement led by the grand mufti Amin al Husseini in the fine arts of communist agitprop, the conveyor of crucial Marxist-Leninist concepts, such as "imperialism" and "colonialism." It pioneered the application of European political categories to the Middle Eastern scene in general, and the Jewish-Arab conflict in particular. Most of the ugly repertoire of modern Arab and Muslim anti-Semitism came from the Soviet Union (with only the racial-biological component added by the Nazis). The CPP taught the Arab extremists the use of Bolshevik rhetorical devices previously unknown. The "anti-imperialism" so imported by the Communists was remarkably ingested by the Muslim extremists, to the point of becoming integral to their conceptions and expression. It merged with*

traditional jihadi views that animated the Arabs of the region.
In the amalgamation of Bolshevism with jihad that turned out
to be so crucial to modern jihad, this was crucial to training
the Arabs in Soviet-style politics. (Laurent Murawiec, The Mind
of Jihad, p. 238)

As Murawiec's last sentence suggests, the Brotherhood's
Palestinian leader learned a great deal about politics from
the Kremlin, and he worked very closely with the Communists
throughout his career. It wasn't only the Nazis who inspired
him; he was a true student of twentieth-century totalitarian-
ism, and he created a toxic poison of Nazi racism—and its con-
crete application—and Soviet Communism. Both elements
were later central to the Ayatollah Khomeini, who similarly
combined German-style anti-Semitism with Soviet methods of
organizing revolution. As Husseini worked with the Palestinian Communist Party to acquire and maintain power, so
Khomeini worked with the Iranian Communist Party—Tudeh—
to overthrow the shah and create the Islamist tyranny we
see today.

There are many important lessons in the history of the
evolution of the concept of jihad in the last century.

First of all, in the years prior to the beginning of World
War II, would-be revolutionaries throughout the world
often borrowed methods and doctrines from both Nazis and
Communists. Don't forget that Hitler and Stalin cooperated

diplomatically and militarily to dismember Poland, and the Nazi-Communist alliance only ended with the German invasion of Russia.

Second, German and Soviet tyrannies had a lot in common, and radical Muslims freely picked elements from each in the creation of a jihadi ideology and the structure of Islamist states, whether the Islamic Republic of Iran or the current Islamic State.

Third, as in the case of Husseini, it is a mistake to look at Muslim tyrants as Middle Eastern versions of a specific Western dictatorship. They are attracted to, and inspired by, earlier totalitarian regimes.

Keep your eyes on that word "totalitarian." That is the key concept.

This also helps clarify the nature of the global alliance we face. The countries and movements that are trying to destroy us have worldviews that may seem to be in violent conflict with one another. But they are united by their hatred of the democratic West and their conviction that dictatorship is superior. So while it may appear that, say, there is little in common between Communist North Korea and radical Shi'ite Iran, or between the leaders of the radical Sunni Islamic State's "caliphate" and the Iranians, in fact it is no more difficult for them to cooperate in the war against us than it was for Hitler and Stalin to cooperate in the 1930s and 1940s.

Not that ideological differences are trivial. Ever since al

Qaeda was smashed in Afghanistan in late 2001, al Qaeda leaders found haven in Iran. This meant that the world's preeminent Sunni terrorist organization had an operational base within the world's preeminent Shi'ite country. That relationship has always been strained, and top al Qaeda leaders have often chafed at having to submit to Iranian discipline. Sometimes bin Laden himself would erupt angrily at the Iranians. Yet, as we learned from documents captured when bin Laden was killed at his secret location in Pakistan in 2011, he received considerable assistance. At a minimum, the ability for al Qaeda terrorists to transit Iran was very useful.

The public would know a lot more about this complex relationship if the Obama administration would permit the publication of the (more than a million) documents seized by operatives of the Sensitive Site Exploitation team at bin Laden's compound immediately following his death. That very important body of information constitutes what a senior U.S. military official calls "the single largest collection of senior terrorist materials ever." (quoted by Thomas Joscelyn and Stephen Hayes, www.wsj.com/articles/stephen-hayes-and-thomas-joscelyn-how -america-was-misled-on-al-qaedas-demise-1425600796)

Disappointingly, only a couple dozen of those documents have been made public, and the Defense Intelligence Agency's numerous summaries and analyses of the files remain classified. But even the public peek gives us considerable insight into the capabilities of this very dangerous global organization. One letter to bin Laden reveals that al Qaeda was working on chemical and biological weapons in Iran. Another document mentions negotiations with the government of Pakistan. Others provide details of operations under way in Africa, and still others speak of preparations for Mumbai-style attacks on European cities. Given the scale of ISIS-inspired or directed attacks we've seen in Europe, in the United States, and elsewhere around the world, I'd say we better smarten up and pay more attention to these and other Radical Islamist statements.

Our guys fighting al Qaeda in Afghanistan and elsewhere badly wanted to know what we could learn from the bin Laden files, and in fact we learned a lot. Contrary to what the administration was saying at the time (during the 2012 election campaign between Obama and Mitt Romney), when the president and his supporters were assuring the American people that al Qaeda was broken and on the run, we learned that their strength had roughly doubled. We were still facing a growing al Qaeda threat. And it was not just in Pakistan, Afghanistan, and Iraq. We saw it growing in Yemen. And we clearly saw it growing in East Africa and elsewhere across North and West Africa. The threat wasn't going away, it was expanding.

The bin Laden documents also show that al Qaeda is extremely attentive to public opinion. Over and over, bin Laden condemns the bloody brutality of other radical Muslim organizations, and he is especially agitated by videos that show the terrorists killing other Muslims. Unlike the Islamic State, which used the videos to recruit thousands of new jihadis, al Qaeda strove to keep a low profile, counting on its doctrine and the effectiveness of its operations to expand. I certainly would not say that al Qaeda is a "moderate" organization. They intend to destroy us and their passion for a caliphate is no less intense than the Islamic State's. While their ideology is the same, the two organizations have different tactics, and time will tell which of them has judged the situation more accurately.

As things stand, we can't have a serious debate about the global war, because our own government won't let the facts reach the American people. The story of the bin Laden documents is just one of many. Some of the information is classified, and properly so, although the current investigation into alleged suppression of intelligence from Afghanistan suggests that politics can trump technical requirements. If Joscelyn and Hayes are right, this is what took place regarding the squelching of the full al Qaeda story. I believe that even—maybe even especially—unhappy stories should be told. I think the American people, who are now called upon to make some terribly important electoral decisions, should have the full picture. For the most part, they are capable of understanding the realities of war, and why even the best military in the history of the world is bound to fail on occasion. In the coming years we're going to have to fight several very tough enemies, and we'll likely lose some of those battles.

Another dramatic example of this Radical Islamic expansion came in the fall of 2007. We witnessed al Qaeda training significant numbers of fighters inside Somalia. Through good intel collection, we watched two separate camps over a six-month period, training approximately 150 terrorists per camp. They had family members at the camp so we were restricted from destroying them, even though we watched their physical fitness training, religious training, and, in one case, their graduation ceremonies. At least a third of the approximately three hundred graduates were white Europeans and a couple of them came from the United States. One of the U.S. trainees actually conducted the first known suicide attack by an American, targeting U.S. forces near a military base in Djibouti.

These fighters weren't part of the local fighting. They were destined for foreign operations. Some in this group of three hundred likely returned to Europe, to the battlefields of Pakistan and Afghanistan, and elsewhere around the world, some likely to Yemen.

Bottom line: al Qaeda got away with it. We allowed them to train their terrorists without destroying these camps. Why? Because of our high legal and moral standards in the rules of engagement. There were family members at these camps, there were "blinks" in our intelligence collection system (we could not get the requisite overhead support, whether satellites, drones, or aircraft, dedicated to this target area). It was all very frustrating. The war in Iraq was raging, things in Afghanistan weren't going very well, and so we weren't as effective as we should have been. Al Qaeda's command and control was eluding us everywhere.

The situation in Iraq was unquestionably part of the reason we couldn't get the detailed information we wanted. The support simply was not available. That's the way life is, quite often. We were losing, General Petraeus was just kicking off his new Surge strategy, and violence levels in Iraq were the highest they had ever been. We needed to show success, and destroying a handful of al Qaeda trainers in a remote corner of the world wasn't important enough.

It still makes me seethe, but this is what al Qaeda does so well. They recruit, find our weaknesses, and exploit them. They used an obscure location in the middle of nowhere in Somalia and trained three hundred operatives for external operations. My sense is that some of those terrorists are out in the world today as sleeper agents, or they are in leadership roles in the various theaters of operation where we currently see Radical Islamists fighting.

If the evidence we have about al Qaeda and other Radical Islamic terror organizations were presented publicly and forcefully, it would be easier for the American people to understand the nature of the war waged against us.

As Joscelyn and Hayes put it,

Making the documents public is long overdue. The information in them is directly relevant to many of the challenges we face today—from a nuclear deal with an Iranian regime that supports al Qaeda to the rise of al Qaeda in the Arabian Peninsula and Islamic State in Iraq and Syria; from confidence-building measures meant to please the Afghan Taliban to the trustworthiness of senior Pakistani officials.

Choosing ignorance shouldn't be an option.

The people would see that we are being attacked by a potent combination of countries and movements. A lot of people miss the key point that the terrorists are strong at least in part because they are getting help from the military and intelligence services of hostile countries. To be sure, the links between the terrorists and the sponsoring countries are sometimes complicated, and just as individual terrorists will cooperate with us for a while and then go back to their anti-American ways, so terrorist organizations will change their allegiance when it seems to their advantage.

People need to grasp that Radical Islam is not primarily about religion—it is about politics. Sharia is the basic legal system derived from the religious precepts of Islam, mainly the Koran and the hadiths (supposedly verbatim quotes of what the Prophet Muhammad said during his life). In its strictest definition, Sharia is considered the infallible law of God. They want to impose a worldwide system based on their version of Sharia law that denies freedoms of conscience, choices, and liberties. Basic freedoms! When one starts messing with freedom of conscience, one is not only violating the U.S. Constitution, but also denying a universal human right. I firmly believe that Radical Islam is a tribal cult and must be crushed. Critics get buried in the details of sunna, hadiths, the umma, and the musings of countless Muslim clerics and imams. These so-called Islamic scholars keep their message so complicated so as to create chaos, to confuse in order to control. Mao, Pol Pot, Stalin, and Mussolini were more transparent. Sharia is a violent law that is buried in barbaric convictions.

Perhaps the scariest part about this to a man who grew up in tiny Rhode Island is that the Organization of Islamic Cooperation (OIC) now says if we criticize the Prophet or Islam, we can be charged with blasphemy. That is like saying as a Roman Catholic (and a St. Mary's School–educated Catholic at that), I cannot criticize the priests who rape and the cardinals and bishops who cover it up!

In a way, we are dealing with the same issues in Islam under Sharia law. The difference is that the Catholics in the United States did not want to apply canon law to the rest of society (although they tried to do this in select cases). Our legal leaders won by arguing that these were secular crimes in a secular world and canon law has no place in the legal process. Muslims want to apply Sharia law by using our own legal system to strengthen what many Americans believe to be a violent religious law that has no place in the United States.

Let us not fear what we know to be true. Let us accept what we were founded upon, a Judeo-Christian ideology built on a moral set of rules and laws. Let us not fear, but instead fight those who want to impose Sharia law and their Radical Islamist views.

4
How to Win

What does "winning" mean and how do we accomplish this against Radical Islamists and their allies? It means several things:

- Destroying the jihadi armies, and killing or capturing their leaders;
- Discrediting their ideology, which will be greatly helped by our military victories, but which requires a serious program all its own;
- Creating a new set of twenty-first-century global alliances. This, too, will emerge naturally from the military and political campaign;
- Bringing a direct challenge to the regimes that support our enemies, weakening them at a minimum, bringing them down whenever possible.

It won't be easy—they're a formidable enemy—and it certainly won't be fast. Indeed, it is impossible with our current leaders, who clearly lack the will and the desire to win.

On the other hand, we know how to win this war. We've done it before, notably in the Second World War and then the Cold War against the messianic mass movements of the twentieth century, Nazism, Fascism, and Communism. Even in the Middle East since 9/11, we've won many battles. In fact, no matter what you've been told about the "lost wars" in Iraq and Afghanistan, we've defeated the Radical Islamists every time we've fought them seriously. Their current positions of strength were not won against us on the battlefield, but were instead the result of our bad, politically motivated decisions to withdraw before victory was consolidated.

The primary requirement for winning any war is the willingness, determination, and resolve to win and to do the necessary things required for victory. At the moment we have a president who said—incredibly, in my opinion—on November 16, 2015: "What I'm not interested in doing is posing or pursuing some notion of 'American leadership' or 'America winning.'"

That says to the American people and to our enemies that America will not lead, does not want to win, and is therefore doomed to lose. Our enemies are certainly determined to lead and to win, whether they are radical Muslims or ambitious secular tyrants.

There is no escape from this war. Our enemies will not permit that. We will either win or lose, and at present we look like losers. Knowing that the current administration will not challenge them, our enemies will press hard to gain every possible advantage before a new president, potentially with the will to win, takes office.

You can see this in Afghanistan. U.S. forces led raids against two huge training facilities in the country's south in October 2015. One of these camps was approximately thirty square miles in size! General John F. Campbell, who oversaw the war effort in Afghanistan between 2014 and 2015, explained that the camp was run by al Qaeda in the Indian Subcontinent (AQIS) and is "probably the largest training camp–type facility that we have seen in 14 years of war." Unbelievable! But sadly, this is not surprising to those of us who have been intimately following this enemy and take them deadly seriously.

AQIS is an important component of al Qaeda; it answers to Ayman al-Zawahiri (an Egyptian), bin Laden's successor. The existence of such an enormous terrorist training facility shows that the terrorists are growing rapidly; it also shows that our intelligence is failing again. AQIS was established in September 2014, and is exporting terrorism throughout the region. The group has claimed attacks in Pakistan and Bangladesh, and al Qaeda is still allied with Pakistan's many jihadi groups, which frequently carry out operations, especially in the northern part of Pakistan.

Think about that: U.S. officials discovered what is probably the largest al Qaeda training camp since 2001. Al Qaeda hasn't been neutralized in Afghanistan. In fact, numerous al Qaeda leaders have relocated into that country.

A few weeks after this training camp was discovered, the Taliban struck a devastating blow just outside our major base at Bagram, where a suicide terrorist on a motorcycle blew himself up, killing six American troops in the deadliest attack in eighteen months (www.thedailybeast.com/articles/2015/12/21/worst -attack-in-18-months-shocks-u-s-military.html?via=desktop&source =twitter).

We were late noticing a huge al Qaeda base, and we were caught by surprise—the worst such attack in a year and a half—by the Taliban. Yet the administration assures us that we're doing well. Eventually we will elect leaders who tell the truth, who want to win, and are able to lead. When these leaders are elected, how should they proceed?

I offer the following four strategic objectives:

- First, we have to energize every element of national power in a cohesive synchronized manner—similar to the effort during World War II or the Cold War—to effectively resource what will likely be a multigenerational struggle. One leader must be in charge overall and accountable to the president—if this leader does not meet the test, which is to win, then fire him or her and find another who can. We have to stop participating in this never-ending conflict and win! And we *must* accept that there is no cheap way to win this fight. The bottom line is that we have to organize ourselves first before we can expect any international coalition to seriously join forces with us to destroy this evil we must clearly define as Radical Islamism.

- Second, we must engage the violent Islamists wherever they are, drive them from their safe havens, and kill them or capture them. There can be no quarter and no accommodation. Any nation-state that offers safe haven to our enemies must be given one choice—to eliminate them or be prepared for those contributing nations involved in this endeavor to do so. We do need to recognize there are nations who lack the capability to defeat this threat and will likely require help to do so inside their own internationally recognized boundaries. We must be prepared to assist those nations.

- Third, we must decisively confront the state and non-state supporters and enablers of this violent Islamist ideology and compel them to end their support to our enemies or be prepared to remove their capacity to do so. Many of these are currently considered "partners" of the United States. This must change. If our so-called partners do not act in accordance with internationally accepted norms and behaviors or international law,

the United States must be prepared to cut off or severely curtail economic, military, and diplomatic
ties. One very precise point on this latter issue. We
tend to blame the Saudis and other Arab nations for
directly funding the Islamic State and other radical
Islamist groups. We must either stop this blame game or
we must provide direct and unequivocal evidence to
the leaders of these nations and offer them one choice
(and one choice only): arrest these individuals and
stop this funding or face severe consequences. And we
must be prepared to back this up. Blaming others for
our own inadequacy does not signal to our enemies,
and more important to our friends, our complete and
total commitment to winning this war against Radical Islamism.

- Fourth, we must wage ideological war against Radical Islam and its supporters. If we can't tackle enemy
doctrines that call for our domination or extinction,
we aren't going to destroy their jihadis. I'll start with
that one, because it underlies our national willingness
to do the others.

We've fought radical ideologies in the past and won. Had
we lost to the Nazis in World War II, much of the world would
be praying at the altar of Adolf Hitler. Omar al-Baghdadi, or
whoever leads the Islamic State, and his ilk of radical ideologi-

cal thugs cannot be allowed to exist in a globalized world that seeks to expand humanity's potential. They want to destroy it.

Waging Ideological War Against Radical Islam

In the last century, we defeated enemies who combined totalitarian ideology with the power of major nation-states. The Axis powers in the Second World War believed their vision of the world, their peoples, and their political doctrines were superior to ours, and they were confident they would overwhelm us. The Nazis' doctrine rested on the conviction that the Aryan race was superior to all others, and consequently a "bastardized" society like ours was unable to resist their unity and intrinsic racial superiority. The Fascists believed they had identified a superior ruling class, composed of those who had performed heroically in the trenches of the First World War and then led the march on Rome in 1922. The Japanese believed their leaders, starting with the emperor, had divine support and were destined to rule the Pacific region.

In the Cold War, we defeated the Soviet Empire and its attendant international Communist movement without a major world war. Both the empire and the movement were inspired by the conviction that they had deciphered the laws of history and that those laws, codified in the doctrines of Marxism-Leninism, guaranteed the success of Communism—led by Moscow—everywhere. When Nikita Khrushchev pounded his desk at the United Nations, or, his shoe at the Polish embassy in Moscow, and threatened to "bury" us he wasn't bragging about the strength of his empire; he was simply and dramatically giving voice (or, in this case, foot) to the core conviction of Communists everywhere.

In each of these wars (World War II and the Cold War), we took it for granted that we had to challenge the enemies' ideology. How could it be otherwise? The wars unleashed against us were waged in the name of our enemies' doctrines, just like jihad today, and both our enemies and we saw the wars as what they were: conflicts of and between civilizations. In the Second World War we constantly warned the American people about the dangers of Nazi and Fascist ideology, critical editions of *Mein Kampf* were published, and speeches by Hitler and Mussolini received outraged publicity. Overseas, our Office of Strategic Services (OSS) waged ideological warfare against the enemy, broadcasting to resistance movements and denouncing numerous and brutal regime crimes, mostly against the European Jewish community. In the Cold War, anti-Communism was commonplace, from the academic establishment to the halls of Congress. The Central Intelligence Agency organized groups such as the Congress for Cultural Freedom that contested Soviet practice and dogma in America and around the world.

These were serious initiatives that engaged some of the

finest minds in the United States. Above all, the campaign against our enemies flowed from the highest levels of the government, starting with the president. These ideological challenges had important consequences. Indeed, they were among the primary reasons for winning the Second World War and the fall of the Soviet Empire.

When most people talk about "war," they think of tanks driving across the desert, planes dropping bombs, ships clashing at sea, and soldiers going toe-to-toe against each other. But at least as important, people need to recognize the strategic power of words and pictures. Our enemies certainly do; they recruit followers and inspire terrorists using words via social media on forums such as Facebook and Twitter, sending their messages of hate across the Internet, which they also use to communicate with their legions of followers, including sleepers in our country. Ideas, and the words that express them, are very much a part of war, but we have deliberately deprived ourselves of using them.

United States citizens and, frankly, citizens of other Western nations should demand that these social media giants become more socially responsible. Why can't Facebook and Twitter start their own positive messaging campaigns about the betterment of humankind? Why can't they seek to maximize the potential of citizens around the world? These mediums are not simply a place to "express yourself" as I was told by executives of one of these companies. My God, if that is what they are for, the world is in deeper trouble than I think. (And I am not naive for one second to think that ugly, despicable, and unlawful behavior can ever be fully eliminated in the information age.) We *must* develop and use twenty-first-century rules and tools differently and stop applying twentieth-century thinking—why can't these giants of the Internet apply their own positive messaging? What are their values based on? This shouldn't require the U.S. government's involvement. If, however, it does, it will require imagination and intellect that more fully and deeply understands how social media provide a voice to the voiceless—especially women and children. We can do better—the social media giants can do better—but if the U.S. government needs to request their support, then those leaders are missing the point of what they truly have: a means to advance humanity in a positive, more enlightened way.

If you have any doubts about the power of words, just look at the campaigns to silence criticism and suppress the truth in enemy countries (both Iran and the Islamic State have banned satellite television, for example), and the amazing mass of lies aimed at us. The jihadis and the secular tyrants know that they must win the ideological war if they are to prevail. For instance, Iranian leaders constantly warn against the dangers of a "velvet revolution"; they know they were very nearly overthrown in the summer of 2009, when millions of Iranians associated with the "Green Movement" filled the streets with more demonstrators than in 1979, when the shah was overthrown.

I saw this potentially world-changing event from right across the border. At the time this revolution was occurring, I was the senior intelligence officer for the International Security Assistance Force in Afghanistan. We were well postured with military forces in both Iraq and Afghanistan, and the people of Iran simply wanted the United States to say we stood with them—they did not want "boots on the ground."

Instead, the Green Movement's leaders reached out to the Obama White House. Some U.S. officials pressed Obama publicly and argued at the Oval Office to back up the movement. Obama's decision was "let's give it a few days." It turns out that the president was invested heavily in secret outreach that year to Khamenei through a channel with Oman. That channel influenced the president's thinking in staying silent. And in 2012 the U.S. set up direct contact with Iran in Oman.

The hapless leaders of the Green Movement have been under house arrest since 2009, the movement itself has been decimated, and, as one of them said recently, "a historic opportunity was missed." In the meantime, the political map of the Middle East has drastically and violently changed. These poor people only wanted our moral support for their cause. It was a severe mistake not to stand up for these freedom-loving

Iranians, whose only desires were to gain a sense of liberty, the simple pursuit of a happier, more stable existence, and a chance for a more prosperous life.

Removing the sickening chokehold of tyranny, dictatorships, and Radical Islamist regimes must be something our nation stands for whenever freedom-loving people around the world need help. If we don't stand for this, we stand for nothing.

We have not responded in kind, to put it mildly. Let's face it: President George H. W. Bush warned against celebrations of the fall of Communism, and President Obama has tiptoed around open criticism of Vladimir Putin's many aggressive actions. As for our major enemy, Radical Islam, ever since 9/11 our leaders have done everything in their power to silence criticism of anything "Islamic," to the point where, until recently, virtually nobody in public life or in academic circles dare speak of Islamic terrorists, even when their motivation was utterly explicit. For instance, many will remember the absurd comments coming from the mayor of Philadelphia, Jim Kenney, in early January 2016, after the Radical Islamist Edward Archer shot the incredibly brave and physically courageous police officer Jesse Hartnett eleven times, severely wounding him. Mayor Kenney stated that in no way, shape, or form did the teachings of Islam have anything to do with the shooting of Officer Hartnett. How would he know this? Is he an Islamic scholar? The shooter himself said he was acting in the name of Islam! If political correctness had not gone amok before this, the mayor's comments certainly made it clear that it now had gone way beyond being irresponsible. Thank goodness that the intellectually honest Philadelphia police commissioner, Richard Ross, called it like it is when he said the shooter took aim to kill Officer Hartnett in the name of Islam. We need more leaders like him.

Amir Taheri (an Iranian-born author) has neatly encapsulated the ideological challenge for America:

- No major power in recent history has gone out of its way as has the United States to help, respect, please, and, yes, appease Islam. And, yet, no other nation has been a victim of vilification, demonization, and violence on the part of the Islamists, as has the United States.

- Criticism of Islam as racist, ethnocentric, or simply vile, [are] all crammed together in the new category, the politically correct crowd, has turned into a new taboo . . . "Islamophobia." Is it Islamophobia to question a religion whose Middle East leaders often preach "Death to America" and hatred for Western values?

- More prevalent than Islamophobia is Islamophilia, as leftists treat Muslims as children whose feathers should not be ruffled. The Islamophilia crowd invites Americans and Europeans to sacrifice part of their own freedom in atonement of largely imaginary sins against Muslims in the colonial and imperialist era.

* Many Muslims resent the kind of flattery that takes them for idiots at a time that Islam and Muslims badly need to be criticized. *The world needs to wake up* [emphasis added]. (www.gatestoneinstitute.org/7092/united -states-islam)

And yet, if ever a deck were stacked in our favor it is this one. We should go after the Radical Islamists with all our energy, using public statements from our top officials, our radio and television broadcasts in their languages, and of course the Internet. As Taheri says, many Muslims—undoubtedly the majority—know they are terribly led, constantly deceived, poorly educated, and used as cannon fodder by the jihadis.

You don't have to send thousands of American troops to defeat Radical Islamic regimes. Properly used, this form of ideological and information warfare can probably bring down the Iranian regime, never mind the sadistic and immoral Islamic State. We should have used this approach instead of invading Iraq in 2003, and we should definitely have done everything possible to support the enormously popular 2009 insurrection in Iran.

The funny thing about the truth is that it fears no questions. The first order of business is to tell the truth about Radical Islamists and their allies, making two fundamental points.

First, the Radical Islamists represent a failed civilization. Second, they are at war with us. It is their war of choice, and they are afraid that if their own people are free to choose the winner, they will choose us, as the Iraqis and the Afghans did at certain stages in each of those wars.

Look at the Muslim world today. It's a spectacular failure. Can anyone remember the last time a scientist, economist, or mathematician in a Muslim country won a Nobel Prize? It did once happen—a Pakistani physicist who trained in Great Britain. The other Muslim laureate, a chemist, spent the bulk of his career at Caltech in the United States. This marks a significant decline in Islamic culture; as the distinguished scholar Martin Kramer rightly says, "had there been Nobel Prizes in [the year] 1000, they would have gone almost exclusively to Moslems."

What went wrong? They banned the search for truth, proclaiming that it had been fully and finally revealed in the Koran. It's impossible—in fact it's heretical—to innovate when you are required to believe that all truth is embodied in a seventh-century text. So it's not all that surprising to find, according to a United Nations study at the end of the last decade, that there were 65 million illiterates in the Arab world (twenty-two countries).

Moreover, those who could read had a very limited selection. Tiny little Greece prints five times more books translated from English than the entire Arab world, and, incredibly, if you add up all the foreign books translated into Arabic in the millennium—that's a thousand years—from the late ninth century to the first decade of this century, the total is less than those translated from English to Spanish in just one year in Spain. And this number doesn't count translations in Latin America. Nor does it count the smattering of books translated from other languages. A full 20 percent of Arabs are illiterate, and many of those who can read have been taught in religious schools, the infamous madrassas, where their learning consists of repetition and memorization of the Koran.

Not only have Muslim countries kept many of their citizens in a state of ignorance of the basic facts about the modern world, they have isolated half the population—the women—from real participation in the society. This is not just a matter of social practice, by which women are kept from the educational system, forbidden to work in mixed environments, forbidden to leave their homes unless accompanied by a close male relative, and subjected to unprecedented levels of sexual violence. Their inferiority is codified in the legal system. In Iran, for example, a woman is defined as being worth half a man. If a pregnant woman carrying a male fetus is killed in an automobile accident, the guilty party is assessed a full penalty for the fetus but only half as much for the mother-to-be.

There is a direct relationship between the fanaticism of the Islamic radicals and the Iranian regime and the misery they inflict on their people. Take Iran, for example, which is the world's leading supporter of jihad and one of the most repressive regimes on earth. On paper, Iran should be one of the richest and most successful countries. It is in a prime geopolitical location, it has abundant natural resources, it boasts a well-educated population, centuries of commercial success, and millennia of high culture. Lucky!

Yet Iran is in ruins. It has undergone an all-time record drop in its birth rate, the corruption of its ruling class is legendary, there are alarming rates of suicide, prostitution, depression, and drug abuse, unemployment is high, and there's a mounting shortage of freshwater. The primary explanation for this historic failure is that the country's wealth is overwhelmingly funneled into jihad and into the private accounts of the nation's rulers and the elitists who continue to steal from the coffers of their people.

The Iranian people know they are suffering, but the regime does its damnedest to hide the details, and anyone who dares speak, write, or use social media to protest is locked away in the country's infamous prisons for years on end. Often they are summarily condemned by a "revolutionary court" and executed. Most Iranians detest the regime and the rulers know it. That is, after all, why repression is getting worse all the time. Executions are up by half under the presidency of the "moderate" Hassan Rouhani. If the Radical Islamist tyrants who rule in Tehran believed they were popular, they wouldn't work so hard to silence their own people.

Nonetheless, the country bubbles with protests and strikes. Iranian women challenge the strict dress code and demand proper education and decent jobs. There is even substantial opposition to the regime among mullahs and ayatollahs. There are thousands of Shi'ite clergy in prison in the holy city of Qom, and many of these are pious believers who are convinced that when the regime inevitably falls, it will bring down Islam along with it.

Despite our perverse current refusal to criticize anything Islamic, those seeking freedom in Muslim countries invariably call out to us for support, knowing that American traditions and values and, eventually, American leadership is their only chance to gain liberty. That is why, in the marches and demonstrations in Iran in 2009, the protesters held signs reading "Obama where are you?" It is why the global Muslim Reform Movement asks for Americans to support their campaign against the imposition of head covering for Muslim women (the hijab—misnamed, as hijab refers to any and all covering of the Muslim woman's body). It is why the various forces combating the Islamic State in Syria and Iraq openly ask for American assistance. From the Kurds to the Free Syrian Army, we, the United States of America, are their hope for salvation.

What are we waiting for? Delay is dangerous to our cause. The people eventually decide revolutionary wars, and if the Muslim masses can't get any support from the United States, they will eventually throw in with the jihadis.

The war against Radical Islamists must begin at home, where we have declined to challenge their doctrines and expose their many failures. As Andy McCarthy, the former prosecutor who led the case against the "blind sheikh" who masterminded the 1993 World Trade Center bombing, writes:

> *Islamic supremacism is not merely the creed of outlier "violent extremists," but of hundreds of millions of Muslims, the ocean in which jihadists comfortably swim. A commander in chief who does not or will not come to terms with those facts is unfit for his most basic responsibilities. His stubbornness renders him incapable of protecting the nation.* (https://pjmedia.com /andrewmccarthy/2015/12/22/obamas-denial-of-the-jihads -ideological-roots-gravely-endangers-the-nation; www.rsis.edu.sg /rsis-publication/srp/co15139-demolishing-the-islamic-state-myth -defeating-the-propaganda-of-isis/#.VkkxwL-4mqj)

We can't win this war by treating Radical Islamic terrorists as a handful of crazies and dealing with them as a policing issue, any more than we can win the global war solely with military forces. The political and theological underpinnings of their immoral actions have to be demolished. Other countries have recognized this, and are acting accordingly. In Singapore, after two "radicalized youths" were arrested, the government worked with the country's Muslim community "by resolving to guide Muslim youth to the correct teachings of Islam."

The government of Singapore correctly recognized that:

The community needed to arm itself with a stronger counter narrative to defeat ISIS' ideology centered on the Islamic State, Caliphate, and emigration. They needed to neutralize the slick propaganda that ISIS is the savior of today's spiritually dispossessed Muslims who come from non-Muslim lands, live under non-Islamic laws, and are ruled by nonbelievers. (http://news.asiaone.com/news/singapore/isis-threat-has-grown -says-dpm-teo)

The government's goal is to get the Muslim community on record that it's quite all right for pious Muslims to live in a secular state, that there is no basis for the radicals' insistence that local Muslims either emigrate to an Islamic state or fight for the creation of one in Singapore, and that there is no requirement that Sharia law be imposed.

Similar efforts are under way in Indonesia, the biggest Muslim country in the world, and half a dozen countries have banned headscarves.

Another more fundamental and dramatic effort would be a call for a complete reformation of the Islamic religion. This must start inside the Muslim community in order to succeed—but it must start somewhere. This need for a "religious" reformation is more for political purposes than purely religious. Radical Islam is a totalitarian political ideology wrapped in the Islamic religion. Why are so many constitutions within the Muslim world based on Sharia, providing for an Islamic regime as an alternative to secular models of governance? Models such as those we have in the West.

As I said with regard to Iran, women who are governed by Sharia have far fewer rights than women in the West. Muslim-majority societies, to varying degrees, have Sharia integrated into their laws, and Muslim families govern their family affairs with Sharia. I found in Iraq and Afghanistan, Sharia courts that imposed vicious judicial punishments on those convicted of various Sharia abuses. These punishments included loss of body parts, hanging in public squares, and in some really sick cases, beheading in front of their families.

With nations such as the *Islamic* Republic of Iran, the Government of the *Islamic* Republic of Afghanistan, the *Islamic* Republic of Pakistan, and other Arab Muslim nations with some form of Sharia at their constitutional foundations, reforming this political ideology is not simply a matter of necessity; it is a vital aspect of changing the behavior of those radicalized by their misinterpretation and flat-out denial of what this ideology does to those who are corrupted by it.

Finally, a call for religious reformation in the Islamic religion was expressed in an incredibly brave and bold speech by the leader of Egypt, President Abdel Fattah el-Sisi, on New

Year's Day 2015. President Sisi has been a vocal supporter of a renewed vision of Islam and he is one who should be internationally admired and respected for his intellectual courage in this call for a reformation of the Islamic religion.

Speaking before Al-Azhar (the scholarly center of Sunni Islam) and the Awqaf Ministry of religious affairs, he made what must be described as the most forceful and impassioned plea by a Muslim world leader to date on the subject of Islamic reformation. Among the many vital points he addressed, he said that the "corpus of [Islamic] texts and ideas that we have sacralized over the centuries" are "antagonizing the entire world"; that it is not "possible that 1.6 billion Muslim people should want to kill the rest of the world's inhabitants— that is 7 billion—so that they themselves may live"; and that Egypt (or the Islamic world in its entirety) "is being torn, it is being destroyed, it is being lost—and it is being lost by our own hands."

Other relevant excerpts from President Sisi's speech that should drive the rest of the Islamic world (religious and secular) to seriously consider and act on his words:

> I am referring here to the religious clerics. We have to think hard about what we are facing—and I have, in fact, addressed this topic a couple of times before. It's inconceivable that the thinking that we hold most sacred should cause the entire umma [Islamic world] to be a source of anxiety,

danger, killing and destruction for the rest of the world. Impossible!

That thinking—I am not saying "religion" but "thinking"— that corpus of texts and ideas that we have sacralized over the centuries, to the point that departing from them has become almost impossible, is antagonizing the entire world. It's antagonizing the entire world!

I am saying these words here at Al Azhar, before this assembly of scholars and ulema—Allah Almighty be witness to your truth on Judgment Day concerning that which I'm talking about now. All this that I am telling you, you cannot feel it if you remain trapped within this mind-set. You need to step outside of yourselves to be able to observe it and reflect on it from a more enlightened perspective.

I say and repeat again that we are in need of a religious revolution. You, imams, are responsible before Allah. The entire world, I say it again, the entire world is waiting for your next move . . . because this umma *is being torn, it is being destroyed, it is being lost—and it is being lost by our own hands.* (www.raymondibrahim.com/2015/01/01/egypts-sisi-islamic -thinking-is-antagonizing-the-entire-world/)

If a Muslim leader of one of the oldest and greatest nations on our planet is calling for a "religious revolution," we must accept, and help lead, the defeat of the jihadis within his own religious and political system. His words are powerful and true.

In order for us to defeat Radical Islam and its allies, a reformation is required.

War of Ideas, War on the Battlefield

Winning the ideological war requires that we also win the shooting war. The two go hand in hand. Our enemies believe they have irresistible support, whether it comes from heaven, or history's laws, or inspired leaders. They cannot imagine losing to us, with our failed (as they see it) and corrupt democratic system, and our hopelessly feckless leaders.

It's an old story. If Marx and Lenin have foreseen the inevitable defeat of capitalism, then it will indeed fall. If the Aryan race is greatly superior to our impure population, then we had better start studying German. Now there's a new certainty that drives the jihadis: if Allah has blessed jihad against America, it cannot fail.

Remember that, just as the Japanese believed they could deliver a devastating blow to us at Pearl Harbor in 1941, Osama bin Laden thought 9/11 would be a knockout punch to America, and he and his successors never stopped working to bring us down. The leaders of the Islamic State and al Qaeda relentlessly identify the United States as their main target, and call for global jihad. Here's the Islamic State caliph, Abu Bakr al-Baghdadi, in December 2015 on the eve of his tactical defeat in Ramadi:

Stand up against the tyrant and apostate people of [the Saudi coalition] and champion your brothers in the Levant, Iraq, Yemen, Afghanistan, the Caucasus, Egypt, Libya, Somalia, the Philippines, Africa, Indonesia, Turkestan, Bangladesh, and everywhere. . . .

The "caliphate's" leader insists that all Muslims are confronted by a "Jewish-Crusader-Safavid alliance that is led by America and was devised by the Jews." From Baghdadi's perspective, the Crusaders include America, Europe, and Russia. Safavid is a derogatory word that is used to describe Shiites and Iran. All of these parties have come together in a coalition to supposedly wage "war on Islam and Muslims." (www.long warjournal.org/archives/2015/12/baghdadi-claims-infidel-nations -are-afraid-of-final-war.php)

Here is Qasim al-Rahmi, the head of al Qaeda in the Arabian Peninsula (AQAP), at virtually the same time, with the same message:

The jihadists should not think of their local battles as the only fight that matters, according to al Rahmi. "We are a single ummah [community of worldwide Muslims] and we are the same people even if we are present in different locations." If one thinks of only himself and "believes in borders," al Rahmi says, then he has "isolated" himself "from the ummah and the [wider] battle."

As the war rages on, the jihadists should "look at the issue from the point of view of a single ummah to find out who is the real enemy," and not from "the standpoint" of stand-alone battlefields in Afghanistan, Iraq, Somalia, Yemen, or elsewhere. From this perspective, al Rahmi argues, it becomes clear that "the true enemy is the American." (www.longwarjournal.org /archives/2015/12/aqap-leader-says-america-is-the-primary -enemy.php)

A global war is being waged against us by all true Radical Islamists in the name of Allah.

What happens if they lose? What does it mean? Defeat at our hands raises some very uncomfortable questions for them, as we saw when we beat al Qaeda in Iraq and the Taliban in key parts of Afghanistan. Al Qaeda (and their Iranian allies) lost favor among potential jihadis. There was an immediate drop in recruitment for al Qaeda in Iraq, and Taliban fighters in Afghanistan sought sanctuary in Pakistan, where they would not have to face the likes of the United States Marine Corps.

We should have taken the ideological offensive, asking whether the Almighty had changed sides in the holy war. After all, if previous victories were the results of divine blessing, were defeats not proof that their cause had been rejected on high?

As in the twentieth century, the military defeat of totalitarian regimes does great damage to their doctrines. Communism lost mass appeal when the Soviet Empire fell. Italian Fascism became an object of ridicule when Italy was defeated on the battlefield; Mussolini went from a leader who "was always right" to the prisoner of an Italian government that joined the Allies; and Hitler was left to proclaim the German people unworthy of him.

The jihadis know this, and they have told their fighters not to be surprised or discouraged if there are military setbacks, as Allah has promised severe challenges for the true believers. It's up to us to make sure they are fully tested.

We must destroy the jihadis on the ground, eliminate their support from friendly or frightened states, and destroy their commercial and virtual networks.

We know how to win on the ground, as we demonstrated in Iraq and Afghanistan. Above all, it requires good intelligence and leaders determined to win. We can't do it exclusively with airplanes and drones; we need our fighting men and women. To be sure, we need to work with local forces—there are plenty of Muslim troops with whom we can profitably ally—but, with the exception of the Kurds (not all of whom are Muslim), they won't be sufficient. Al Qaeda bases and all the territory claimed by the Islamic State must be destroyed and returned to local control, and we must insist on good governance—not, as we have so often done, turning it all over to the locals and accepting yet more "Islamic republics." It's not just a matter of changing local leaders; we want to change the whole system as we used to do.

We will only be safe and secure when others are safe and

secure, and we are facing a complete breakdown of order in the region. Our own history teaches us that we were a nation built on an idea and that idea was to be free, to live our lives based on life, liberty, and the pursuit of happiness. That can only be accomplished in an orderly society.

Although it is a pipe dream or a president's "willing ignorance" to believe we can bring full democracy to this region in the near future, we could certainly bring order.

As we do that, we need to have some tough love conversations with the leaders of countries who pretend to be our friends, but who also collaborate with our enemies. Countries like Pakistan need to be told that we will not tolerate the existence of training camps and safe havens for Taliban, Haqqani, and al Qaeda forces on their territory, nor will we permit their banks and other financial institutions to move illicit funds for the terror network. They are going to have to choose, and if they continue to help the jihadis, we are going to treat them harshly, cutting them off from American assistance, and operating against enemy safe havens.

The same tough approach applies to the financing of the jihadi network. Over the years, the terrorists have raised a lot of money from individual donors (sometimes contacted in person, other times online), but criminal activities are a much more important source of money. Some of the best intelligence work carried out by the American government has been done in this area. We can thank the Drug Enforcement Agency (DEA) and the Treasury Department, along with the CIA, and especially our FBI and local law enforcement organizations such as the New York City Police Department, one of the outstanding counterterrorist organizations anywhere. Their intelligence shows that terrorists and common criminals work together very closely, having created an underground railroad of spectacular sophistication and size. Drugs, money, and weapons are moved between North and South America, West and sometimes North Africa, the Middle East, and Europe.

If you look into this underground railroad, you will find the usual suspects: terrorists, the countries that support them, and drug cartels and criminal opportunists of every species.

As I noted in early 2010, in an article (https://mail.google.com /mail/u/0/#label/urgent/151e4488b9dc4eb3?projector=) coauthored with Simone Ledeen, the merging of narcotics traffickers, organized criminals, and terrorists was produced by the availability of and access to money. They traffic in drugs, arms, human beings, and even weapons of mass destruction. It's imperative to deprive these groups of access to easy money, in order to weaken and eventually break the deadly alliance between terrorists, conventional criminals, and the states that support them both.

Just ask the Iranians, who have been desperately trying to break the grip of sanctions on their banks and trading companies for years. The Iranian proxy, Hezbollah, has been particularly active in the terror-criminal network, as demonstrated by the activities of the Barakat brothers in the South American Tri-Border Area.

In the spring of 2014, Brazilian police arrested Hamzi Ahmad Barakat and accused him of embezzling money from fellow Lebanese immigrants, and creating false documents to create companies to cover for trafficking in arms and drugs. According to press accounts, Barakat sent the proceeds of his various illegal activities to Hezbollah. He put the well-known Brazilian gang "First Capital Command" in contact with weapons dealers in the Tri-Border region between Brazil, Argentina, and Paraguay, where there are between 7 and 13 million Lebanese. The region is a Wild West area, and is infamous for corruption, loose border controls, and several Mafia-type organizations.

Hamzi's brother, Assad Ahmad Barakat, was arrested in Brazil in 2004, extradited to Paraguay for tax evasion, and sentenced to seven years in jail. Assad Barakat, who has been identified by the U.S. Treasury Department as one of Hezbollah's most prominent and influential members (indeed, the Paraguay police described him as the terrorist group's military commander in the region), raised some $50 million for the terrorist organization in the five years before 2001 (of the roughly $100 million sent to Hezbollah in that period).

The story of the Barakat brothers is typical of the nexus between organized crime and organized terror. There's a lot of money to be made in the terror business, and it is an even greater incentive than Radical Islamic doctrines. In Iraq at the beginning of this decade we found that fully three quarters of those involved in the terror network were in it for the money rather than religious convictions.

As is so often the case when looking at the battlefield, I also found a Russian connection. When the Soviet Empire fell, there were a lot of unemployed KGB officials scrambling to make a living. They were a perfect fit with the terror networks, had few moral compunctions about cooperating with violent anti-American organizations (they'd been doing it for decades), and over the next few years many of the KGB's safe houses, station headquarters, and secure communications networks were put at the disposal of terror groups.

The addition of the former KGB officers gave the network of terrorists and criminals a big boost in professionalism, but I knew a great deal about the individuals involved, and knew the U.S. had our own professionals who were highly skilled in tracking the flow of funds and the movement of arms, drugs, and captive women. I certainly wouldn't say that the KGB connection helped us map the enemy network, but it did offer us an additional window into their world and it also gave us many opportunities that we should now exploit even more vigorously.

As the U.S. Intelligence and Law Enforcement communities document the details of the connections between terrorists, drug dealers, money launderers, and traffickers in human beings, it adds to our arsenal against them, both in terms of law enforcement and the ideological war. Exposing such unsavory connections gravely undermines the Radical Islamists' claim to piety and moral standing. It is difficult for them to argue that Allah has blessed the efforts of drug dealers and the like. As the common criminals among them are rounded up and imprisoned, we should publicly point out there is very little religious virtue involved in such activities. As of the end of 2015, the Islamic State was primarily funded by such activities: extortion, oil smuggling, kidnapping, and so on.

There is a lot to be done, but there are signs of progress. There is now an international counter-ISIS group, and its first meeting was held in March 2015, jointly chaired by Saudi Arabia, the United States, and Italy. Perhaps the members will benefit from a viewing of a recent documentary—*From Russia with Cash*—on the massive flows of cash into London, New York, and Miami. A lot of it gets invested in luxury real estate:

The numbers are staggering. Annually, $1 trillion is stolen by corrupt officials from countries around the globe. That money needs to be spent, or laundered, and much of it goes into big anonymous real estate deals in the United Kingdom, which is seeing £1 billion in unrecorded capital inflows per month. The main source of that money? Russia. (www.atlanticcouncil

.org/blogs/new-atlanticist/from-russia-with-cash-dirty-money
-unchecked-in-london#.VnnrUJ1Ov8g.twitter)

It is impossible to say with confidence how much of that cash (£1 billion per month in the U.K. alone) is involved in terror finance, but with a trillion dollars a year stolen by and from corrupt countries, it's safe to assume the numbers are significant.

There is also a lot to do in the digital universe. Earlier, I wrote about my beliefs of what the social media giants should be doing. We have long known that al Qaeda uses the Internet to distribute recruiting videos, send messages to its followers, criticize and intimidate its rivals, and distribute coded instructions to terrorists. Al Qaeda set a precedent for the other jihadis, and ISIS seems to have moved the bar even higher. The rapid expansion of the Islamic State is unprecedented, and its success is due at least in part to its skills online.

According to the International Centre for the Study of Radicalisation and Political Violence, the territory controlled by ISIS now ranks as the place with the highest number of foreign fighters since Afghanistan in the 1980s, with recent estimates putting the total number of foreign recruits at around 20,000, nearly 4,000 of whom hail from Western countries. Many of these recruits made initial contact with ISIS and its ideology via the Internet. Other followers, meanwhile, are inspired by the group's online propaganda to carry out terrorist attacks without traveling to the Middle East. (www.atlanticcouncil.org /blogs/new-atlanticist/from-russia-with-cash-dirty-money -unchecked-in-london#.VnnrUJ1Ov8g.twitter)

ISIS and al Qaeda use the full array of digital technology, from Web sites and chat rooms to slick video productions and effectively encrypted messaging. It was only at the end of last year, to take perhaps the most recent deadly example of the use of text messaging to organize terrorist attacks, that French authorities revealed to *Le Monde* that the frightful slaughter in Paris on November 13, 2015, was coordinated from a single cell phone in Belgium, used solely for that purpose. The Belgian phone was activated the day before, at 10:24 p.m., and at 9:21 on the evening of the 13th it received a short text message from the Paris group headed for the concert to begin their attack: "We're on our way, it's starting." Within two minutes, the phones were shut off.

The French phone was found in a garbage can outside the concert hall where an American group, Eagles of Death Metal, was featured. The concert hall attack as well as two others that same evening in Paris were coordinated via text from the same phone in Belgium. As of this writing in April 2016, the user has still not been identified.

Even the best technology can't save us from well-organized

killers. Unless there were other communications leading up to the 13th of November, there's no digital technology that would have alerted Parisian authorities to the operation. We'd have had to infiltrate the group and known in advance about the attacks. Since we still don't know who was on the line in Belgium, this obviously didn't happen.

Nor should you believe that intercepts of terrorists' communications are necessarily reliable guides to their real intentions. In the War on Terror, for example, some of our top analysts came to believe that the Iranians were deliberately sending us misleading messages via what we believed to be real phone calls. Since the Iranians thought we were listening to most all of their conversations, it would have been to their advantage to muddy the intelligence waters. Technology will only take you so far; a trained and cunning mind is always necessary in these matters.

Some believe that if we could thoroughly map the ISIS and al Qaeda digital networks, we would be able to monitor all the potential terrorists, but even this is overly optimistic. Oddly, in the United States it is not illegal to recruit or indoctrinate online; we have to wait until some "real" crime, such as traveling (or organizing a trip) from a Western country to terrorist training camps overseas, is committed. Our law enforcement agencies have done quite well at coping with such restrictions.

Moreover, there's an ongoing dispute within the intelligence community about the best use of the digital information. It's similar to the kind of disagreements that inevitably crop up on the battlefield and in traditional espionage: some will always want to destroy any clearly identified enemy target, or arrest known hostile agents, while others will feel that the intelligence value of watching our enemies at work exceeds the gain from temporarily putting some of them out of business. Hostile digital operations are extreme cases of this dilemma, since it is so easy to create new sites online.

My own view is that, once again, the truth is the most lethal weapon against Radical Islam. While some of this digital warfare (breaking their codes, identifying some of their sites in the so-called dark web, and tracking terrorists' communications) must be done secretly, the bulk of it, the part that has to do with the ideological conflict, is best defeated by exposure. When potential followers and recruits become aware that we are watching sites to which they are attracted, many of them will be scared off. Knowing or believing that the Radical Islamists are under constant observation undercuts their appeal and sabotages their prestige.

At the moment, various governmental entities are engaged in the creation of a coherent strategy to defeat the jihadis in the digital universe. These entities include U.S. Cyber Command, Homeland Security, the State Department, the FBI, operating under a plethora of legal authorities under Titles 10 (Armed Forces), 50 (War and National Defense), and 22 (Foreign Relations). Each will have its own reading of the relevant statute, and each will attempt to accumulate control over as much bureaucratic turf (and federal money) as they can. This must cease and we must operate as one cohesive team focused on a single goal—winning the global war against Radical Islam and its allies (www.defenseone.com/ideas/2015/12/us-needs-someone -run-effort-defeat-isis-online/124664/).

Digital war necessarily involves the private sector as well. No doubt many citizens were surprised to learn that the metadata collected by the National Security Agency is actually held by private companies, and we can't possibly have an effective campaign against Radical Islamic ideology without the cooperation of the likes of Google, Facebook, and Twitter.

Our cyber army therefore contains governmental and private forces, along with others from the military and civilian sectors. What are all these guys doing? Nobody should be surprised to learn that many of them are doing the same as many of the others, and, inevitably, they sometimes make embarrassing mistakes.

For instance, at the end of 2015, Twitter, following a false claim in the *New York Post*, suspended the account of Iyad el-Baghdadi, a popular blogger and leader of the Arab Spring. Twitter and the *Post* had confused him with the caliph of the Islamic State. The blunder was quickly corrected, and, while certainly embarrassing, I rather suspect that it may well have had a positive effect—to cause more serious understanding of the enemy we face.

With such a large body of major players, we badly need effective organization—otherwise the organizations will constantly bump into one another—and skilled leadership. Somebody's got to define the basic mission and decide who does what. As I said earlier, find an effective leader, place that person in charge and if the person doesn't work out, get rid of him or her and find another who can do the job. Abraham Lincoln's Civil War model is probably the best historic example. He kept relieving his generals until he found Ulysses S. Grant, who went on to win the war (and eventually became our eighteenth president). Lincoln was one of our very best presidents—wish we had leaders like him today.

A serious question that must be answered is, Do we want to shut down the most radical Web sites or concentrate our efforts at exposing them, and then challenging their doctrines?

The multiplicity of actors involved further complicates the situation. Shutdown of the [enemy] networks and Web sites and takedown of [their] propaganda and material for example, will involve the private sector including social media and Internet service providers (ISPs). . . . The idea would be to encourage nongovernmental entities to hunt and gather pertinent information that could be turned over to ISPs, thereby helping them to marginalize the most egregious content. . . . The EU's [European Union] new Internet Referral Unit refers potential terms of service violations to providers in order

to reduce the amount of extremist content online. (www
.defenseone.com/ideas/2015/12/us-needs-someone-run-effort
-defeat-isis-online/124664/)

Defeating messianic mass movements was our mission for
most of the twentieth century. We had to fight them at all
levels and by all means. We had to defeat their armies, the better
to demonstrate that their defeat was inevitable, and that the
power of the master race, and the laws of history, weren't good
enough against the United States of America. We displayed our
economic, military, and political superiority. So complete was
our victory that some very smart people believed—at least for
a while—that history itself had come to an end, that the superiority of the American model was so complete that a frontal
challenge was unimaginable, and that henceforth war itself
would be limited to economic competition.

   The Radical Islamists and their allies did not believe that
history had come to an end, nor did they think that the American model was destined to dominate the world. Indeed, at the
end of the Cold War, at the very moment the Soviet Empire
was headed toward defeat, they were organizing what they
believed would be our inevitable defeat at their hands. Al
Qaeda was the first major global jihad organization, and
Osama bin Laden believed that we could be eliminated as
a superpower in a single stroke. Now there are so many of
these organizations—notably ISIS—that only an expert with

near-total recall can keep track of them all. They are well-funded, well-armed, well-trained, and confident that they can do us in. It would be foolish for us to wait until they pose an existential threat before taking decisive action. Doing so would only increase the cost in blood and treasure later for what we know must be done now.

Not surprisingly, the recent congressional draft Authorization for Use of Military Force, or AUMF (a minor component of a still-required comprehensive strategy), signals that we are willing to wait for them to become existential. Again, this is irresponsible and dangerous thinking.

Instead, this authorization should be broad and agile, with clearer and more decisive language and unconstrained by unnecessary restrictions. These restrictions cause not only frustration in our military and intelligence communities but they also significantly slow down the decision-making process for numerous fleeting opportunities. If this is due to a lack of confidence in our military and intelligence leadership, get rid of these leaders and find new ones.

If there is not a clear, coherent, and comprehensive strategy inclusive of all elements of national power forthcoming from the administration, there should be no new authorization at all; simply leave the existing one in place.

There are solutions to this problem. However, solving tough, complex problems such as eliminating Radical Islam from the planet will require extraordinary intellect, courage, and leadership. Leadership that isn't obsessed with consensus building; instead, leadership that is tough-minded, thoughtful, patriotic, and, when it matters, decisive.

We will have to shed some of the feel-good doctrines that have constrained us in recent years. One of the most unfortunate of these is known as the Powell Doctrine, named after General Colin Powell. According to this view, we should never use military power unless there is a strong domestic consensus in its favor. This, General Powell hoped, would greatly reduce the possibility of a large antiwar movement that would inevitably shackle our war effort.

Colin Powell is a great American, but the doctrine is backwards. The consensus that matters is not the one that exists at the beginning of fighting, but the one at the end of the war. If we win, our leaders will be hailed, while if we lose, they will be despised. Things have not changed much since Machiavelli told his prince "if you are victorious, the people will judge what ever means you used to have been appropriate." Winners are always heroes and losers are almost always . . . losers.

Military leaders like to say that while planning is very important, no plan survives the beginning of actual hostilities. We need leaders who accept that life is full of surprises and that we all make many mistakes. One of our greatest wartime presidents, Franklin Delano Roosevelt, remarked that when things go bad in life you should junk whatever strategy you had adopted and get a new one. However, he stressed, it was vital to keep making decisions until you found a strategy that worked.

We have seen this type of leadership throughout world history and we have examples in our own travails, typically at the most dangerous moments—from George Washington, Abraham Lincoln, and FDR to Ronald Reagan. When faced with threats to our way of life and the lives of our friends and allies around the world, they stepped up to lead. Whether that meant forcing our will on the enemy or outmatching them with our wits and imagination, they faced the difficult reality head-on. While he will not be considered one of our greatest presidents, George W. Bush had the insight and courage to change our strategy in Iraq. Our current leaders have not admitted that their original plans were mistaken, and have not changed their actions accordingly.

I had the privilege and pleasure to serve under an outstanding leader, General Stanley McChrystal, and his maltreatment is still hard for me to digest. I honestly thought that cooler heads would prevail back in Washington and that he would have his ass chewed out and told to get back into the fight and stay out of the media for a while (even though Stan was rarely in the media). The *Rolling Stone* article was based on junior officers' comments and not due to some "frat house atmosphere" that Stan created—that is totally false. If anything, Stan was the greatest disciplinarian that I have ever worked around. His demanding style was amazing and his level of professionalism displayed at all times was difficult to equal. He never allowed any antics other than light kidding of each other and his own self-deprecating humor about himself. Speaking about politicians was simply not something he would *ever* allow, and did not. The comments attributed to him (secondhand) were surely misleading, but (unlike former secretary of state Hillary Clinton) Stan took full responsibility for everything that took place within his command.

Everyone involved with McChrystal knew the truth. The secretary general of NATO, Anders Fogh Rasmussen, came out with a supporting statement almost immediately, well before President Obama decided to remove McChrystal. Many of us expected the president would come to the same conclusion, especially when we learned that both Defense Secretary Robert Gates and Admiral Mike Mullen, the chairman of the Joint Chiefs of Staff, recommended that Stan be retained. We were actually starting to have some effect in Afghanistan, and the newest campaign plan was just starting to take hold. The president, however, had other considerations.

Although the secretary general of NATO obviously doesn't decide which military commander the United States will choose, in the case of McChrystal's ouster, Rasmussen wasn't even informed.

Back in Afghanistan, the moment the decision was announced, many in the HQ were literally crying. It was as though we had just lost the war, never mind simply losing a commander (and we knew that General Petraeus, a noted leader in his own right, would replace him). Many senior officials in Afghanistan were afraid that Petraeus would change the strategy and fall back on his experiences in Iraq (keep in mind that at this time he had very little experience in Afghanistan).

I lost a friend and the nation lost a great leader who understood how to defeat this enemy better than anyone else, as has been demonstrated ever since.

America is a big country and great leaders can certainly be found among our more than 300 million citizens. As we tackle this grave crisis, we must hope that the political process will give us good choices and that the U.S. electorate will then choose wisely.

Conclusion

It may well be that we are no longer shocked or horrified by the slaughter of innocents by jihadi terrorists. There have been so many videos, photos, and descriptions of suicide bombings, beheadings, mass executions, public hangings, and even stonings, that they have become part of the background noise of our world. We have heard them say "we love death more than you love life" over and over again, and we have heard them chant "Death to America." Yet it does not seem that our leaders, and perhaps not even most of our people, are sufficiently moved to fight decisively against the barbarians who act in this way. Political correctness forbids us to denounce radicalized Islamists, and our political, opinion, and academic elites dismiss out of hand the very idea of waging war against them.

No wonder we're losing. They've gotten a free ride.

Perhaps if we go back to an earlier event in the war, nearly half a century ago, we can recapture its essence and make the threat we face more urgent. I'm totally convinced that, without a proper sense of urgency, we will be eventually defeated, dominated, and very likely destroyed.

We've got to get inside the minds of the jihadis. We should have done that a long time ago, because their goal has been clear for nearly half a century.

On November 28, 1971, the Jordanian prime minister was shot to death by PLO assassins in a Cairo hotel. As he lay dying, "one of his killers bent over and lapped the blood that poured from his wounds."

As Laurent Murawiec has written in *The Mind of Jihad*:

Inseparable . . . from contemporary Islamic terrorism are the idolization of blood, the veneration of savagery, the cult of killing, the worship of death. . . . The highest religious authorities sanction or condone it, government authorities approve and organize it, intellectuals and the media praise them. From one end of the Muslim world to the other.

Do you want to be ruled by men who eagerly drink the blood of their dying enemies? Such questions are almost never asked. Yet if you read the publicly available ISIS documents on their intentions, there's no doubt that they are dead set on taking us over and drinking our blood. It's not just a fight for a few hundred square miles of sand in the Syrian, Iraqi, and Libyan deserts. They want it all as evidenced by this quote from a leader in ISIL:

"Accept the fact that this caliphate will survive and prosper until it takes over the entire world and beheads every last person that rebels against Allah. . . . This is the bitter truth, swallow it." (www.usatoday.com/story/news/world/2015 /07/28/ami-isil-document-pakistan-threatens-india/30674099/)

What will our lives be like if we lose this war? It's actually a very easy question to answer: we'd live the way the unfortunate residents of the "caliphate" or the oppressed citizens of the Islamic Republic of Iran live today, in a totalitarian state under the dictates of the most rigid version of Sharia. A Russian KGB or Nazi SS–like state where the citizens spy on one another, and the regime doles out death or lesser punishment to those judged insufficiently loyal.

We can see such a system in place in the Islamic Republic of Iran, and in the ISIS caliphate. The facts about Iran are well known. In the case of ISIS, we know this system was planned from the beginning. In the summer of 2015, the German magazine *Der Spiegel* published a set of plans for the creation of the caliphate, beginning with the takeover of existing towns and cities (www.spiegel.de/international/world/islamic-state-files-show -structure-of-islamist-terror-group-a-1029274.html).

The process of creating an internal security system was very detailed. The population would be invited to religious services, and one or two of the most pious recruited. They were to be instructed to collect information on their neighbors, including:

- Provide lists of the powerful families.
- Name the powerful individuals in these families.
- Find out their sources of income.
- Name names and the sizes of (rebel) brigades in the village.
- Find out the names of their leaders, who controls the brigades, and their political orientation.
- Find out their illegal activities (according to Sharia law), which could be used to blackmail them if necessary.

The spies were told to note such details as whether someone was a criminal or a homosexual, or was involved in a secret affair, so as to have ammunition for blackmailing later. "We will appoint the smartest ones as Sharia sheiks," Haji Bakr had noted. "We will train them for a while and then dispatch them." As a postscript, he had added that several "brothers" would be selected in each town to marry the daughters of the most influential families, in order to "ensure penetration of these families without their knowledge."

The man who drafted this wiring diagram of the Islamic State, Haji Bakr, was well trained for his mission; he'd been a colonel in Saddam Hussein's Air Force Intelligence Service, which meant he'd worked with his Soviet bloc counterparts. The documents discovered by the *Spiegel* journalists were typical KGB-style products, and Haji Bakr had no doubt embraced the Sharia code and the requirement of piety that Saddam had authorized in the last decade of his tyranny.

ISIS does not hesitate to kill its own people, even its fighters, if they prove unworthy of the caliphate's mission:

> *ISIS fighters who fled to the terror group's Iraqi stronghold of Mosul after being defeated in Ramadi were burned alive in the town square, sources told FoxNews.com, in an unmistakable message to fighters who may soon be defending the northern city from government forces. Several residents of Mosul recounted the grisly story for stateside relatives, describing the deadly reception black clad jihadists got when they made it to Mosul, some 250 miles north of the city retaken by Iraqi forces operating with cover from U.S. air power.*
>
> *"They were grouped together and made to stand in a circle," a former resident of northern Iraq now living in the U.S. but in touch with family back home told FoxNews.com. "And set on fire to die."*
>
> *Several Iraqi-Americans and recent refugees with close relatives in Mosul told of ISIS fighters fresh off defeat in Ramadi being shunned—and executed—for not fighting to the death in Ramadi.* (www.foxnews.com/world/2016/01/12/isis-burns-fighters-alive-for-letting-ramadi-fall.html)

That's what we'll get if we lose this war, along with all the grim censorship we see in groups such as the Islamic State, al Qaeda, and the Taliban or from nations like Iran, North Korea, and Cuba. In the Islamist lands, there is no singing, women are covered up and mostly kept at home, no women are permitted in public unless chaperoned by a male relative, no unofficial public gatherings, no criticism of the rulers, no freedom or praise of it, public executions to keep everyone suitably terrified, and terror attacks or full-fledged military assaults against those unbelievers surviving outside the caliphate.

Our lives are deeply involved with entertainment, but the Islamist regimes, of the sort our enemies intend to impose on us, are devoted to the destruction of fun and beauty. Remember that when the Taliban ruled Afghanistan, music was forbidden, and in Iran today citizens are forbidden to sing in the streets, and even poetry has been widely banished and poets singled out for punishment. In October 2015, two leading Iranian poets—one of them a woman—were sent to jail for six and eleven years, plus one hundred lashes, for writing poems the judge didn't like. Islamic judges and prosecutors don't need hard evidence to punish such people, because they can read the writers' minds!

The Tehran Islamic prosecutor, however, insisted that [Fatime] Ekhtesari's "ambiguous poems" were meant to pass "dangerous political messages that could encourage people to distance themselves from the True Faith." "She writes something but means something else," the prosecutor claimed. "Her trick is to avoid saying anything in a straightforward way, creating space for all manner of dangerous thinking." (http:// english.aawsat.com/2015/11/article55345600/iran-where-poetry-is-a -national-crime)

In addition to the prison sentences, the poets' books were banished, and the poets themselves removed from even virtual society. They cannot be named in public or print, nor can photos of them appear either online or on a real page. As famous English writer and poet Dr. Samuel Johnson so eloquently stated, "poetry is the art of uniting pleasure with truth." Today, people in Iran cannot tell the truth about the evil that exists inside of their Islamic Republic—and this inability to do so makes them (and us) less likely to enjoy the true pleasures that life brings.

The Islamic State's intention has been well described by the Italian writer Maurizio Molinari, the author of one of the best books on ISIS:

> *The caliphate is characterized by three features: the reference to the origins of Islam . . . the great common land of the Arab peoples of the Middle East; an ideology centered on the use of absolute violence against enemies—Shiites, Christians, Jews, and all Sunnis who do not think like them; and then, the state project, the will to create a state.* (www.cmc-terrasanta .com/en/video/the-caliphate-history-and-the-threat-of-terrorism -summarized-in-a-book-8583.html)

Radical Islamists intend to create an even larger Islamic state based on the ancient precepts of Radical Islam, and they are fully prepared to use absolute violence to achieve it.

The Islamic State and associated terrorist movements are highly inefficient in many ways; however, they are very disciplined when it comes to killing and silencing their enemies, especially within their own domains. It is no accident that Radical Islamists in America are pushing very hard and very systematically to gain legal standing for Sharia, and to forbid any and all criticism of Islam; these are all steps toward creating an Islamic state right here at home. We have to thwart these efforts and encourage criticism of those who support them. There are many American Muslims who have spoken out against the advance of Radical Islam in the United States, and they are predictably singled out by the Islamic radicals in our country and, to a degree, shunned by politically motivated people in our own government. As in all aspects of the war, this is not merely a matter of intellectual debate. Ayaan Hirsi Ali, an incredibly courageous Muslim woman and a celebrated author and activist, is forced to hire bodyguards lest her radical opponents fulfill one of their countless death threats against her.

If we cannot criticize the radical Muslims in our own country, we cannot fight them either in America or overseas. Unless we can wage an effective ideological campaign in the United States, we will not be able to defeat the jihadis on foreign battlefields, because we will not understand the true nature of our enemy. Long ago, Sun Tzu explained that is a prescription for certain defeat.

You can see our determination to avoid charges of "Islamophobia" by looking at the rules of engagement under which we fight in places like Afghanistan. Eli Lake, a no-nonsense writer, describes it this way:

> "There are real restrictions about what they can do against the ISIS presence in Afghanistan," Mac Thornberry, the chairman of the House Armed Services Committee, told me about the rules of engagement for U.S. forces. . . .
>
> Thornberry said that the rules of engagement, combined with what he called micromanagement from the White House, have led military officers to tell him they have to go through several unnecessary and burdensome hoops before firing at the enemy.
>
> "My understanding is it's a very confused, elaborate set of requirements," Thornberry said. "I think the effect of going through all of that makes it harder for our people to conduct their missions."
>
> He would not get into specifics about the rules, saying, "If the public were able to know all the restrictions placed on our troops, they would be unhappy about it, and if the enemy knew this they would have more of a leg up than they do now." (www.bloombergview.com/articles/2016-01-12/rules-of -engagement-in-afghanistan-limit-u-s-effectiveness?utm

_campaign=trueAnthem:+Trending+Content&utm_content
=5696a5ba04d3011752388ea9&utm_medium=trueAnthem
&utm_source=twitter)

This is very dangerous, I know. Rules of engagement (or ROE) are, by their nature, classified, in order to keep our enemies from knowing when we might kill or simply wound them. But ROE must also be simple and easily understood. That is not the case on today's modern battlefield, and that is too bad because it restricts our soldiers and Marines from doing what they are very well trained to do—close with and destroy our nation's enemies.

Remember the oft-quoted line from our own Battle of Bunker Hill (Boston, 1775), "Don't fire till you see the whites of their eyes!" Meaning, "Don't use any of your gunpowder until they're really, *really* close, so you won't miss." Now that's clear ROE. And I'm certain, as that whispered command made its way through the ranks, that the men standing on the line of liberty all clearly understood what they needed to do that day to destroy their enemies. Those who courageously led that day on the field of fight realized that clarity of purpose and simple language for those militiamen were required. We need that same clarity of purpose today.

In short, we are not fighting to win in Afghanistan, or on any battlefield. We're training and advising the locals, and when our soldiers find themselves in combat, they are constrained by rules of engagement that limit their ability to defend themselves properly.

When it comes to Iran, it seemed we were actually delighted when the naval forces of the Revolutionary Guards captured two of our ships and detained ten U.S. sailors, forcing them to kneel and clasp their hands behind their heads, as took place in mid-January 2016. The Iranians publicly declared this to be proof of their country's great power, while the White House and State Departments pronounced it a sign of the wisdom of their diplomatic and strategic embrace of the Islamic Republic.

That sort of shameful behavior can only encourage our enemies to take further steps against us. If they have no fear of the U.S. Navy (the head of the Revolutionary Guards said they had targeted our aircraft carrier, the *Truman*, as well as a French carrier, and would have destroyed them both if we had attempted to respond to the capture of our ships and sailors), what then can restrain them?

Moreover, the effect on our troops is devastating. Who wants to deploy when your commander in chief will celebrate your capture by our worst enemy? Who wants to volunteer to serve in a military that is routinely blown up by terrorists and rounded up by the world's leading sponsor of terrorism?

It's a real crisis. We faced a similar crisis in Iraq in 2009, and the White House changed its strategy from Surge to withdrawal, but didn't provide the necessary military resources we required to maintain decent security and sustain hard-fought victory. The intelligence community did not adapt quickly enough and for political and bureaucratic reasons is not adapting today. There has to be an entirely new strategy, and intelligence must drive this, as it has driven successful American efforts on the battlefield since 2001. Good intelligence has to start with properly and clearly defining this enemy. If we don't have that, we are likely to fight this conflict for generations to come. We should be challenging the assumptions we have—they are obviously incorrect assumptions, because nothing we are doing seems to be a winning strategy.

Our credibility is nonexistent right now. Our reputation as a military force and our ability to train effective fighting forces in the Middle East is in question. Our intelligence assessments are also in question. Our top intelligence officers are accused of falsifying the picture of the war in Iraq, Syria, and Afghanistan, and they failed to spot, early on, the biggest al Qaeda training camp in Afghan history. Nor are our elected representatives any better; it took three years before the Benghazi terrorist attack on our diplomatic compound attracted big-time public attention, and the key event was a movie, not the kind of aggressive congressional investigation warranted by the assassination of an American ambassador.

This is not a good place to be after nearly fifteen years of this persistent, never-ending war. We have to stop half-assed participation, repeatedly deploying token forces year in and year out, and we must win!

We must drive change in our institutions and driving this change takes intellectual bravery, not just the physical courage our soldiers display daily on the battlefield. Our leaders in Washington, from the White House to the Pentagon to our major military headquarters, have proven they aren't up to it.

We are fighting an enemy that wants to win, legitimately believes they are winning, and is bringing the war to our homeland. We need a winning strategy.

When developing a strategy you have to do the following:

1. Properly assess your environment and clearly define your enemy;
2. Face reality—for politicians, this is never an easy thing to do;
3. Understand the social context and fabric of the operational environment;
4. Recognize who's in charge of the enemy's forces.

We're not doing any of those urgent tasks very well. We can't define our enemy, not because we're unable to do it, but because our political leaders won't permit it. Years from now this will seem utterly astonishing.

The 2015 attacks in Paris, France, San Bernardino, California, across the nation of Israel, and the early 2016 suicide bombings in Jakarta, Indonesia, Istanbul, Turkey, and Brussels, Belgium suggest that the old approach to containing terrorism has collapsed, along with the credibility of the leaders who advanced it. More than 30,000 people died in terror attacks in 2014, compared to fewer than 8,000 in 2011. Another example comes in 2015, when our very own director of national intelligence stated there were approximately 20,000 foreign fighters from roughly eighty countries fighting in Syria. Only a year later, the newly designated special presidential envoy to the Global Coalition to Counter ISIL (as ISIS is also known) Brett McGurk, during an early January 2016 interview, stated, "The world has never seen something like this, upwards of 35,000 *new* foreign fighters from 100 countries all around the world supercharged by social media and Twitter and everything. It's something we've never seen before."

Something is seriously wrong and our U.S. strategy to defeat ISIS is clearly not working.

We must face the reality that we are in a crisis. The people of the United States are duly scared or at least uncertain about the outcome (just look at the incredible increase in gun sales for self-protection). The attacks in our country will happen again and again until we crush this enemy. Let's stop participating in this never-ending nonsense, call it and our enemy what they are, war and Radical Islam, and let's win!

Attacking the Enemy Alliance

The two most active and powerful members of the enemy alliance are Russia and Iran, and we can judge their efficacy in the skies and on the ground in Syria and Iraq. It's an odd partnership, to be sure, since President Vladimir Putin of Russia knows that he faces a serious threat from Radical Islamists inside his own Russian Federation borders, of which Iran is the world's leading sponsor.

Indeed, Putin himself oversaw the infamously brutal slaughter by Russian security forces of radicalized Islamists during a ferocious assault of a secondary school in early September 2004 in the small community of Beslan, North Ossetia. Here is where over 1,100 people, including 777 children, were being held hostage by a group of armed Islamic terrorists, mostly Ingush and Chechen. The siege by the Islamists lasted three days and finally ended with the assault of the school and the massacre of at least 385 of the hostages, including 186 children.

It was so vicious that it prompted David Satter, a former *Wall Street Journal* correspondent who has written extensively about Russia, to write for the Hudson Institute: "President Putin's determination to crush the Chechen resistance at all costs is a form of moral suicide that will destroy what is left of Russian democracy and could threaten the whole world" (www .hudson.org/research/3538-slaughter-in-beslan).

Whatever Putin's cooperation with the Iranians in the fighting in Syria and Iraq, and on Tehran's nuclear program, his own people provide a remarkable number of volunteers for ISIS. Less than a year ago, Yevgeny Sysoyev, the deputy director of the Russian intelligence service (FSB), publicly revealed that between 20 and 25 percent of the 20,000 foreign fighters who have joined ISIS in Syria have come from post-Soviet states, many of them from the Russian Federation.

Like our own "experts," the Russians do not well understand Radical Islam, and the jihadis have exploited this ignorance to the point where one of the country's true experts on Islam has shown that official government policies in essence pay for the growth of the radical organizations.

In an interview published in *Moskovsky Komsomolets*, Aleksey Grishin, the president of the Religion and Society Analytic and Information Center, said that "unfortunately, many of the Russian officials . . . know so little about the religion that extremists are able to twist them around their fingers and in fact get the Russian state to finance and otherwise support what are extremist activities.

Islamist radicals . . . routinely come to these officials and propose cooperation. The officials out of ignorance or in some cases out of corrupt considerations agree, the expert says, and as a result, the extremists are integrated into and supported by the state."

As a result, "Islamist organizations of the most doubtful kind conduct on [Russian] territory at [state] expense forums, print extremist literature, and conduct under subversive activity against the foundations of the state," Grishin says.

The Islamists are further assisted in their work by . . . the great age of the majority of rural mullahs and imams and the multiplicity of and competition among the Muslim spiritual directorates (MSDs).

Almost three quarters of rural imams in Muslim regions of Russia are elderly, older than 70 or 75. The extremists use this. They appear in the villages, gain the trust of the elderly imams, offer to help them, read prayers, and provide regular assistance to the indigenous Muslim community.

That allows them to disseminate their extremist materials via the mosques. And "when the imam dies, who replaces him? Of course, these people." (www.interpretermag.com/russia -and-other-post-soviet-states-supplying-twenty-percent-of-foreigners -fighting-for-isis-fsb-says/)

The same sort of incoherence dominates Putin's counter-terrorist operations, with a welter of agencies and ministries forever getting in each other's way. That gives the jihadis the chance to spread death throughout the North Caucasus:

> [Rasul] Kadiyev says in an article on the site Kavkazkaya Politika that the recent events in Derbent where forces, which claimed to be part of ISIS, attacked and killed some local

people "confirm that mistakes in providing security" reflect the
difficulties the Russian authorities are having in coordinating
their counter-terrorist actions.

As a result, he says, the FSB, the National Anti-Terrorist
Committee, the Ministry of Defense, its various special groups
and regional staffs, the various regional and republic govern-
ments, and the Russian Information Monitoring Agency are
often working at cross purposes rather than [as] a single team.
(www.interpretermag.com/moscow-struggling-to-coordinate
-counter-terrorist-effort-in-north-caucasus/)

Therefore, when it is said that Russia would make an ideal
partner for fighting Radical Islam, it behooves us to remember
that the Russians haven't been very effective at fighting jihadis
on their own territory, and are in cahoots with the Iranians. In
Syria, the two allies have loudly proclaimed they are waging
war against ISIS, but in reality the great bulk of their efforts
are aimed at the opponents of the Assad regime. They are
certainly not "fighting terrorists" in the Middle East; theirs
is a battle to rescue an embattled ally in Damascus.

Although I believe America and Russia could find mutual
ground fighting Radical Islamists, there is no reason to believe
Putin would welcome cooperation with us; quite the contrary,
in fact.

In mid-January 2016, the Kremlin announced its intention
to create new military bases on their western border, and to

step up the readiness of their nuclear forces. These are not the actions of a country seeking détente with the West. They are, rather, indications that Putin fully intends to do the same thing as, and in tandem with, the Iranians: pursue the war against us. The other alliance members do, too.

The Iranians are the heart of the alliance, and they are vulnerable. Machiavelli insisted that tyranny is the least stable system, because the people can quickly turn against the tyrant. Khamenei knows that, and lives in constant fear of a "velvet revolution," a popular uprising that will sweep him away, along with the failed Islamic system created by his predecessor. We can best attack the enemy alliance at its weakest point, the failure of the Iranian Revolution. That attack should be political, not military, and our most potent weapon is what Khamenei most fears: the suffering Iranian masses.

It was a huge strategic mistake for the United States to invade Iraq militarily. If, as we claimed, our basic mission after 9/11 was the defeat of the terrorists and their state supporters, then our primary target should have been Tehran, not Baghdad, and the method should have been political—support of the internal Iranian opposition.

Is it too late? Has the Iranian opposition been decisively crushed? Many think so. But then, many thought so in 2009, before the massive antiregime demonstrations erupted after the fraudulent elections. Perhaps the Iranian people have the courage to challenge the regime again. We should at least consider how to change Iran from within, remembering that such methods brought down the Soviet Empire, certainly a mission more daunting than bringing down the Islamic Republic.

If internal opposition could end the role of the last president of the Soviet Union, Mikhail Gorbachev, why not Khamenei's?

Nothing of the sort will be undertaken by the Obama administration, because this president wants to be remembered as the man who embraced the Islamic Republic, not as the American leader who brought it down. Our challenge to the mullahs and their allies in the Kremlin will have to await new leadership in Washington. Those new leaders will have to craft a winning strategy that will bring freedom to Iran, thwart Putin's ambitious undertakings in the Middle East and Europe, and break the worldwide enemy alliance.

Assembling Our Forces

We are not without resources. Although our enemies are strong and growing stronger, and although our military and economic strength has been gravely weakened in recent years, we can win this thing. But only with good leaders capable of galvanizing the country, restoring morale and better intelligence to the military and the intelligence community, and establishing new and rebuilding our current international alliances. Our new leaders are going to have to undo the alienation of traditional friends from Europe and the Middle East to South Asia and Latin America. Diplomacy alone will not be sufficient; at the moment, nobody takes us seriously. We will have to demonstrate the ability and the resolve to crush our enemies.

We should start with strengthening our relationships with Israel, Jordan, and Egypt. Israel is the only country in the world that routinely defends itself against terrorist attacks—when most of the world refuses to call it terrorism. The Israelis live next to terrorist states, and are constantly asked not to treat them as threats, but to make generous concessions to them.

Israel is enormously valuable to us. Israeli intelligence organizations are exceptionally good, their understanding of Radical Islam is very deep, and their technology may be the best in the world. Of the many mistakes of the Obama presidency, its open hostility to Israel is one of the most damaging to our national security. I find it simply incredible that an American president should believe a strategic alliance with Iran to be more attractive than our traditional embrace of Israel. Our new leaders need to reverse that, pronto. We will need Israel if we're going to defeat the Radical Islamists, and above all, the Iranians.

Egypt is the biggest Arab country, which saved itself from the clutches of the Muslim Brotherhood. I have quoted at some length from President Sisi's brave call for a Muslim "Reformation," and he well understands the urgency of destroying the jihadi armies in Libya, Gaza, the Sinai, and Yemen, as well as doing everything he can to fight the Brotherhood inside Egypt. If we are to defeat al Qaeda and ISIS in North Africa, Egypt is indispensable. Here, too, we must reverse policy.

Jordan has long been the one Arab country to really make peace with Israel, and Egypt has joined their ranks. King Abdullah's kingdom is now doubly threatened: hundreds of thousands of refugees have headed to Jordan from the Syrian and Iraqi wars, and the Jordanian government lacks sufficient money and supplies to deal properly with them. Second, the Iranians and Syrians are supporting terrorist attacks, and although Jordan has a first-class intelligence community, they can certainly use additional help.

We need to support the Jordanians any way we can, and our Middle East strategy should be coordinated with all three of these nations. We will also want to undo the severe damage that has been done to our relationship with the Saudis, who will have to deal with an intensifying Iranian campaign in the immediate future.

We will also need to revive our working relations with countries such as Poland, Hungary, the Czech Republic, India, and Argentina. Long-standing friends such as Australia, Great Britain, France, Germany, and Italy will be easier, but there's an awful lot of hard work to do.

Good, strong diplomacy will be indispensable, but you can't undo years of dithering and retreat with words alone. We will have to take real steps, we will have to take action on the battlefield. I don't want to make specific tactical recommendations here, because the situation is changing so quickly, and good leaders are always ready to abandon a losing strategy in favor of something more promising.

We wouldn't have a country at all if our first commander in chief, General George Washington, hadn't been willing to try something dramatically new at the darkest hour of the Revolutionary War. At the beginning of 1781, the British were clearly winning, having defeated the French in Rhode Island and Americans in the South, and were in firm control of New York. Washington was broke, unable even to pay the cost of delivering supplies to his soldiers, and was receiving intelligence to the effect that the French were on the verge of bailing out.

The intel reports were wrong (sound familiar?). The French commander, Count de Rochambeau, told Washington that money was coming from Paris. He also suggested a change in military strategy: instead of concentrating on New York, it would be better for the Americans to coordinate with the French navy in the Chesapeake Bay, and Rochambeau's own ground troops against General Charles Cornwallis. Over the course of the next several months, General Cornwallis moved his British troops south to Yorktown, Virginia, and Washington quickly agreed with the French to spring a trap. First, the French navy thwarted British efforts to relieve Cornwallis. Second, the Marquis de Lafayette kept Cornwallis in place. And third,

Washington committed his troops to a joint operation with Rochambeau. That was the battle of Yorktown, won decisively by the French-American forces in October. It marked the effective end of the Revolutionary War.

That is what good leadership is all about. We want the world, very much including our own people, to see that we are effective and determined to prevail. We will do whatever it takes to win, and we're prepared to rethink our strategy at all times. If they see it, those who share our values will join with us to win the global war against Radical Islam and its allies. But I don't think we can win without them. Like Washington at Yorktown, we will need help.

As we enter the field of fight, we must never forget the firm convictions of our enemies. The man who created al Qaeda in Iraq and laid the groundwork for the Islamic State, Abu Musab al-Zarqawi, wrote their motto: "The spark has been lit here in Iraq, and its heat will continue to intensify—by Allah's permission—until it burns the crusader armies in Dabiq." Dabiq is a town in Syria where a famous Ottoman Empire battle occurred in 1516, and where the leaders of the Islamic State expect the decisive battle between themselves and the West to take place. That is why they named their monthly publication "Dabiq."

We killed him in Iraq, now we must destroy the global jihad he spawned.

Suggested Reading

Ansary, Tamim, *Destiny Disrupted: A History of the World Through Islamic Eyes*. New York: PublicAffairs, 2010.

Bar, Shumel, *Warrant for Terror, The Fatwas of Radical Islam and the Duty to Jihad*. Lanham, Md.: Rowman & Littlefield, 2006.

Beck, Glenn, *It Is About Islam: Exposing the Truth About ISIS, Al Qaeda, Iran, and the Caliphate*. New York: Threshold, 2015.

Cleary, Thomas, *The Art of War: Sun Tzu*. Boulder, Co.: Shambhala, 1988.

Finkel, Caroline, *Osman's Dream: The History of the Ottoman Empire*. New York: Basic Books, 2007.

Gabriel, Brigitte, *They Must Be Stopped: Why We Must Defeat Radical Islam and How We Can Do It*. New York: St. Martin's Press, 2008.

Gertz, Bill, *The China Threat: How the People's Republic Targets America*. Washington, D.C.: Regnery, 2002.

Gorka, Sebastian, *Defeating Jihad: The Winnable War*. Washington, D.C.: Regnery, 2016.

Hamid, Tawfik, *Inside Jihad: How Radical Islam Works; Why It Should*

Terrify Us; How to Defeat It. Mountain Lake Park, Md.: Mountain Lake Press, 2015.

Hopkirk, Peter, *The Great Game*. New York: Kodansha International, 1992.

Ledeen, Michael, *Accomplice to Evil: Iran and the War Against the West*. New York: Truman Talley Books, 2009.

———, *The Iranian Time Bomb: The Mullah Zealots' Quest for Destruction*. New York: Truman Talley Books, 2007.

———, *The War Against the Terror Masters: Why It Happened. Where We Are Now. How We'll Win*. New York: St. Martin's Press, 2003.

——— and W. H. Lewis, *Debacle: The American Failure in Iran*. New York: Knopf, 1981.

Murawiec, Laurent, *The Mind of Jihad*. Cambridge, Mass.: Cambridge University Press, 2008.

Nakash, Yitzhak, *The Shi'is of Iraq*. Princeton, N. J.: Princeton University Press, 2003.

Naylor, Sean, *Relentless Strike: The Secret History of Joint Special Operations Command*. New York: St. Martin's Press, 2015.

Patai, Raphael, *The Arab Mind*. Tucson: Recovery Resources Press, 2010.

Quataert, Donald, *The Ottoman Empire: 1700–1922*. Cambridge, Mass.: Cambridge University Press, 2005.

Rashid, Ahmed, *Descent into Chaos: The U.S. and the Disaster in Pakistan, Afghanistan, and Central Asia*. New York: Penguin, 2009.

Weiss, Michael and Hassan, Hassan, *ISIS: Inside the Army of Terror*. New York: Regan Arts, 2015.

Zakaria, Fareed, *The Future of Freedom: Illiberal Democracy at Home and Abroad*. New York: Norton, 2003.

Index